IT'S YOUR MOVE

BY FRITZ RIDENOUR

Illustrator: Joyce Thimsen
Editorial Research: Georgiana Walker

G/L
REGAL
BOOKS
TM

A Division of G/L Publications
Glendale, California, U.S.A.

Printed in U.S.A.

Published by
Regal Books Division, G/L Publications
Glendale, California, 91209, U.S.A.

Library of Congress Catalog Card No. 73-120783
ISBN 0-8307-0081-1

One must train the
habit of faith. C.S. LEWIS

Contents

A teaching and discussion guide for use with this book
is available from your church supplier.

FOREWORD

*Here's how you
can play
"It's Your Move"*

For many people, under and over thirty, a major portion of the Bible remains a closed book because they think something like this:

"The Old Testament? All those stories about Noah's ark, Joseph's coat, David and Goliath? Fun for little kids maybe, or little old ladies cramming for their 'finals.' To me, it's all a real drag."

But . . . is the Old Testament a drag or just **undiscovered?** There is some pretty terrific stuff in the Old Testament—with real human interest. The Biblical record talks about ordinary people with ordinary (and extraordinary) hang-ups, but there is an added unique ingredient. Only the Bible tells us how God fits into man's rather muddy picture, from the very beginning until now. To be more precise, the Bible fits man (mud and all) into **God's picture.**

The question is, how do you dig out all that human interest drama? Abraham, Jacob, Moses, Joshua . . . they're all tremendous personalities, but they suffer from what might be called "overexposure." They have been the subjects of so many sermons, Sunday school lessons and Bible story books that they have a sort of plastic coating of unreality.

But suppose, just suppose, you could play a little game with some of these Bible characters, a game called, "It's Your Move."

How do you play? Simple. In each chapter of this book you put yourself in the sandals of Noah, Moses, Jonathan, Elijah, Joshua—twelve Old Testament characters in all—as they face dilemmas and problems that test their faith in God.

Each chapter opens by talking about a basic hang-up that most of us wrestle with daily. Some examples: Be selfish or generous? Admit you're wrong or cover up? Take revenge or forgive? Give up or keep going? After a page or two, you have the opportunity to step back into Bible history to match wits and courage with one of the "super-heroes" of the faith. In fact, you **become that character,** so to speak, as you trace his career up to a crisis point in his life. Sometimes the crisis is dramatic, sometimes it seems rather minor, but always it's a question of faith.

Trust God or doubt Him? **That** is the issue. And, instead of just going by the script (the Biblical record of what actually happened), you stop to ponder a few options, and their possible consequences. (Surely, being human, that is what these Old Testament men must have done.)

As you decide for or against a certain course of action, you are more than a spectator watching God's drama of redemption roll across the Bible's pages. You become a participant. You get down to the nitty-gritty meaning of faith.

At one level faith means accepting certain doctrines or beliefs. But there is another level to the Christian faith. That higher level deals with **what you do** and **who you are** because you share your life with God in Christ.

And after you wrestle with what you would have done had you been Abraham, Joseph, Samuel, Jeremiah, etc., you step back into **now** and do some hard thinking about how you will live out **your** faith in the space-age rat race. And that is what this book and this little game is really all about—helping you be honest about your faith and how you live it. Are you ready? It's your move.

FRITZ RIDENOUR,
Youth Editor

CHAPTER 1

LORD, I BELIEVE!

HELP MY UNBELIEF!

Keeping the faith is definitely approved behavior in Christian circles. Whether you come in through the Cradle Roll door or join the church as a teenager or adult, you constantly hear about the need to "have faith."

Jesus talked a lot about faith. He was always looking for even the tiniest bit of faith in those He taught and helped.

On one occasion a father brings his demon-possessed son to Jesus. The boy foams at the mouth,

1

gnashes his teeth, refuses to eat. Jesus asks the father how long the child has been this way and he replies, "Since he was very small. The demon often makes him fall into the fire or into the water. Oh, have mercy on us and do something if you can."

"If I can?" Jesus asks. "*Anything* is possible if you have faith."

And then comes the father's classic reply: "I *do* have faith; oh, help me to have more!"

That was all Jesus needed. He cast out the demon and the child was healed on the spot. (See Mark 9:17–27, *Living New Testament*.)

The story has a happy ending, but you can't help but wonder if maybe the father was "putting Jesus on" just a little. After all, according to one Bible translation, he said, "I believe, help my *unbelief*."

But aren't we all like this father? We all "have our doubts." We're not always too sure just how much faith we really have—in people, products or even in God. Oh yes, we like to sound confident, but the doubts are still there:

Yes, we "believe" the old jalopy will make it to the beach and back one more time (if the timing chain holds and right rear tire doesn't blow).

We "believe" that driver sees us in the crosswalk and will stop (if he isn't fiddling with his radio).

We "believe" the doctor knows what he's doing, and when he cuts us open, he'll get us back together again (minus any sponges).

We "believe" a certain product will work well or last long (didn't the salesman say it would?).

Life quickly teaches us that machines, schemes, and people aren't to be trusted completely. It's

natural for the father of the demon-possessed boy to have doubts, even when Jesus looked him in the eye and said, "*Anything* is possible if you have faith."

The father wanted to believe. He desperately wanted his child to be well. But he still "doubted" that this fellow called Jesus could really do anything. And so he was honest and said exactly what was on his mind: "I believe, but I don't believe all the way. Help me believe more."

The father's honest cry of anguish "says it all" for every one of us. From Adam until now, God has given us opportunity to believe in Him. The Bible is a record of our response to God, how we (the human race) have chosen to doubt Him or trust Him.

For example, take Noah and his ark. Noah's story has been told so often in Sunday school lessons or sermons that we sometimes slip into the error of not taking it too seriously once we hit high school or beyond.

Now just for example... suppose you had been Noah and God asked *you* to build an ark...

4

But suppose you had been in Noah's shoes. Nobody knows exactly when you lived but it was a long time ago. It was a time of incredible idolatry and immorality. It was a time of great rebellion against God. (Come to think of it, all this isn't too hard to imagine, is it?)

One day, apparently out of the clear blue, God communicates with you and tells you to build an ark because He plans to destroy all life with a flood. (See Gen. 6:13,14.) Now, if you lived near the sea, this would seem like a reasonable task. You could build the ark near the edge of the water and get some friends to help you shove it in. But you live many miles from any kind of body of water big enough to float an ark. Furthermore, it seldom rains where you live.

"Now honestly, Noah, what *do* you think of all this?"

In his imaginative monologue, comedian Bill Cosby catches some of the spirit of incredulity that Noah must have felt. According to "Cosby's version" of Genesis, there Noah is, sawing away in his rec room, making a few things for the home, when suddenly a voice thunders, "Noah!" Cosby (Noah) pays little attention but the voice repeats itself and says, "It's the Lord, Noah!" Cosby looks around, gets a silly smirk on his face and says, "Right!" The Lord goes on to say that He wants Noah to build an ark. Noah replies again, with an "I'm really hearing things" look on his face: "Right!" and goes right on to ask, "What's an ark?"

Finally Noah can stand it no longer and blurts out: "Who is this, *really?*" And a little later he asks the Lord, "Am I on 'Candid Camera'?"[1]

Cosby's imaginative display of 20th century skepticism might sound a bit flip, but is he really so far off? Noah was a human being—just like you. What would *you* say if a voice spoke out of nowhere and said, "It's the Lord, Noah." ("Right!" ???)

What would *you* say if the Lord commanded you to build an ark because He was going to destroy all living things with a flood?

("Right!" ???)

Did Noah obey the Lord's command without even a second thought? Not necessarily. Had you been Noah you might well have pondered some options. For example, why not plan an evangelistic effort to get all the people to reform so God wouldn't have to send a flood.

This doesn't sound like a bad idea. In fact it sounds downright noble and self-sacrificing. Trou-

6

Noah... you must have thought about...

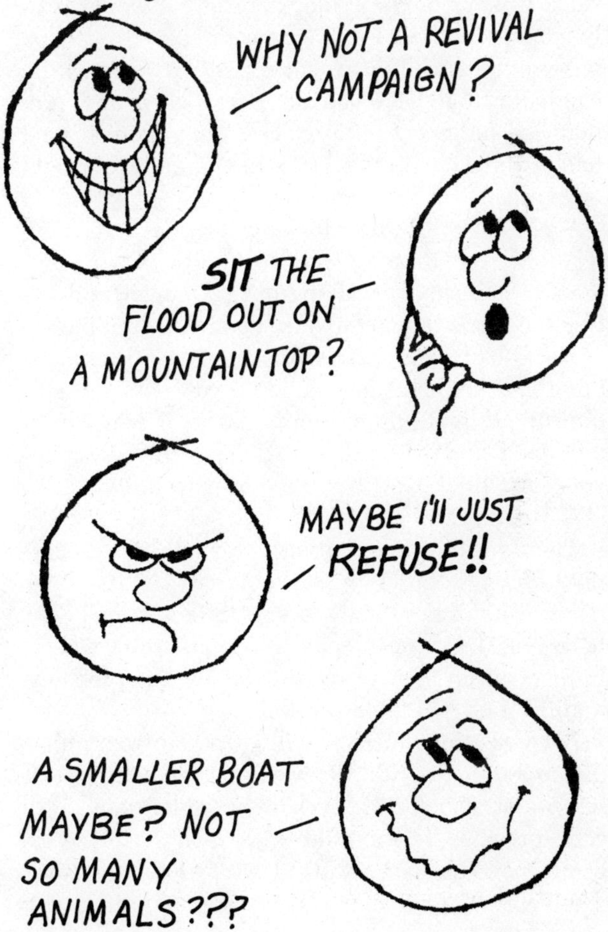

ble is, it's a typical trap that many a Christian falls into. This trap is the habit that many of us have of saying in so many words to God, "Your idea is OK I guess, God, but I've really got a better one and since I understand my idea and how it would really work, why don't I use it instead?"

Yes, you could have suggested an evangelistic campaign, but God had already spoken and pronounced judgment on a wicked generation. If God had wanted an evangelistic campaign, He would have asked you to conduct one.

Well, if we "scrub" the evangelistic campaign, what do you think of the possibility of you and your family simply walking out of danger and sitting the Flood out on top of some high mountain?

Not a bad idea . . . except, can you find a mountain that's high enough? God told you He's going to destroy *all* living things with a flood. It will pay to take God at His word. To do less will be saying you don't think God has the power to do what He says He'll do.

There's a third fascinating option. Why not simply refuse to build the ark? What will God do then? To disobey God's orders might sound like heresy at best, suicide at worst. (If you've been brought up in Sunday school, this idea is probably unthinkable. Still, it's a possibility.)

But two strong motives will keep you from refusing to build the ark: (1) very natural feelings of self-preservation and even more important, (2) your previous relationship with God has been a good one. You have "walked with God," meaning that you and God share love, companionship, etc.

8

In other words, Noah, you and God are real friends and you are well aware of God's power and purpose.

There are other options. For example, instead of building a huge boat (at least the size of a modern day destroyer) you could build a smaller craft that would hold just you and your family. That would certainly save a lot of chores every morning and night. (As Cosby says on his record, "Who's going to clean up that mess down there?") But again, that would violate God's clear-cut instructions—so many cubits long, so many cubits wide, so many cubits high, so many animals, two by two. (See Gen. 6:14–21.) God has made His will explicitly clear, Noah, and in the final analysis you have one of two choices: obey or disobey, believe God or doubt Him.

Now as most people know, Noah did build the ark but if you're interested in the details on how he did it and what happened, see Genesis 6–9 or turn to page 159.

All right, it's been sort of fun "being Noah" for a few minutes (especially when you aren't really facing any floods or having to build any arks). But what *is* your approach to obeying God, to having faith in Him in a space age when it is said that all truth is relative, when some people talk like God is a worn out idea that was useful for comforting superstitious clods who lived before the scientific breakthroughs of the twentieth century?

Perhaps you "really hear" the young person who wrote the prayer on the next page ... •• • •

I feel like such a Fool trying to believe

Lord, I feel such a fool talking to you . . .
trying to believe.

I'm not sure if you're listening . . . or laughing . . .
or sleeping . . . or if you're there at all!

I may as well be screaming at the wind.
My words just blow away . . . drift away and die.

But the silly thing about it is that
I keep thinking about you!

You slip through my doubts
like a chink of light . . . like a haunting secret!

If only I could be positive and really believe!
I don't have faith like that . . .
something solid and certain!

All I have is a funny feeling.
It's the kind of feeling you have when you think
you've met a certain person before, but you can't
quite visualize the face or the time or the place.

Yet somehow you know this person knows you well.
And you could scream because you can't quite open
the door and meet that person face to face.

Sometimes he seems so close that
you could flick him with your eyelashes . . .
if only you could see him clearly.

And then you catch yourself talking to him again.
And you say to yourself:

"I feel such a fool talking to you, Lord,
trying to believe."[2]

10

When you know the Faith, you express the Faith [3]

Or at least so somebody has said. Since it's the scientific age why not experiment with faith just the way the research boys work with nuclear physics or biochemistry? They are constantly testing their theories to see if they work. You can do the same with that "theory" called faith.

Maybe you need to really begin at the beginning . . . with Bible reading, prayer, going to church. Maybe you've been doing at least that much for years . . . it doesn't matter.

What does matter is that *you act as though God is really there.*

11

Talk to Him . . . tell Him about your doubts. If you feel like a fool for trying to believe, admit it (He knows). Ask God to help you with the problems of each day, big ones and little ones.

Try praying (not saying) the Lord's prayer and *meaning* it. Live as if God is there and you'll find out that He is a fact, not a theory. But He won't become fact until you experiment . . . until you experience Him.

Maybe you're pretty sure God is, but nothing much is happening spiritually for you. The same principle of experimenting applies. You've got to go into action. Get in motion. No one can guide a bicycle that is leaning against the wall. But you *can* guide a bicycle that's moving. God won't guide you if you're always standing still, paralyzed by doubt and misgiving. Step out, try things, get moving, make your mistakes. God will guide you in correcting them.[4]

As the title of this book puts it: "It's your move." Why not take a few minutes and a scrap of paper and plan some personal experiments of faith. Try God and see what will happen. Come to Him honestly and pray: "Lord, I believe . . . through my own puny experiments help me to believe more."

Make your move . . . and never fear . . . God will make His.

It's my move

○ I would describe my
personal relationship to God as:
close _____
cordial _____
polite _____
cool _____
indifferent _____

○ Some faith experiments I
want to try:

_____

_____

_____

_____

Things Jesus said about faith
that I want to think about:
Matt. 9:27-29; Luke 7:1-10;
○ 17:5,6; John 10:29.

CHAPTER 2

In the late 1960's Glen Campbell made it big on the pop music charts with a catchy little number called "Less of Me." Young and old responded enthusiastically to the "golden rule" ideas that Campbell talked about—being a little kinder and a little blinder to the faults of others. Being willing to praise others more, being a little more cheery when you feel weary, and, in general, thinking a little more of others and a "little less of me."

One of the basic ideas that most people have about Christianity is that being a Christian means that you will be the kind of person who thinks a little more of others and a little less of yourself. While this isn't the keystone of Christianity, it certainly is one of the all-important building blocks.

The keystone of Christianity is a personal relationship to God through Jesus Christ by repenting of sin and receiving Jesus Christ as Saviour from sin and Lord of your life (John 1:1–12; 3:1–17; Rom. 10:9,10). Out of this relationship to God, which causes you to become a new creation and a new person (II Cor. 5:17), come the basic attitudes that Glen Campbell sings about in "Less of Me."

The Bible teaches that to try to tack attitudes of kindness, love, etc., onto your sin-ridden nature is useless. Working your way to heaven has nothing to do with becoming a Christian (Eph. 2:8,9). Doing good works because you know Jesus Christ, does (Eph. 2:10).

The old hymn tells us to trust *and* obey. Or, as James put it: "Faith that doesn't show . . . good works . . . is dead and useless" (James 2:17, *LNT*).

Getting those good works done is where the rub seems to come in. Sure, we trust God, and we want to obey Him, but it's so easy to look out for number one and put all the rest (including God) second (which really means last).

Big and little names in the Bible have wrestled with this one. They were very human, really, and their experience with God proves things haven't changed that much. In chapter 1 you had a taste of

15

playing Bible VIP (Noah) when you pondered just what you would have done if God had dropped in to tell *you* to build the ark. But that was just for openers. Now that you're warmed up . . .

Why not try Abraham on for size?

SUPER BELIEVER

Now, if you think Abraham isn't too easy to identify with, you probably aren't alone. After all, he's the one that a lot of Bible storybooks build into something of a "superbeliever." Yes, he was the one who was willing to leave the civilized but idolatrous comfort of his hometown (Ur of the Chaldees in Mesopotamia) and journey hundreds of miles west to Canaan—all on the strength of "a call from God."

Yes, Abraham was the one who was willing to believe he and wife (Sarah) could have a child

when they were both far too old. And Abraham
was the one who was willing to sacrifice that child
(his only son, Isaac) when God asked him to. Yes,
it seems that Abraham stacks up as a man who apparently never had a doubt and never slipped an
inch in his chrome-plated, one-hundred carat walk
with God.

Not quite. You see, there are other stories—
lesser-known incidents that help us get a better
look at what kind of a person you really are, Abraham. For example, when you came out of Mesopotamia and finally got to the wild western frontier
of Canaan you ran smack into big trouble—famine.
And so you headed for Egypt, "the breadbasket of
the ancient world" where grain crops seldom fail
because of the water available from the Nile River.

Now, so far you've been willing to go along with
what God said back there in Mesopotamia when
He "called you out": "Leave your own country behind you, and your own people, and go to the land
I will guide you to. If you do, I will cause you to
become the father of a great nation; I will bless
you and make your name famous, and you will be
a blessing to many others" (Gen. 12:1,2, *Living
Books of Moses*).

But God hadn't mentioned famine and here you
are about to go into the strange and not necessarily
friendly territory of Egypt in order to stay alive.
You've heard a little bit about Egyptian tastes in
women, and you're well aware that your wife Sarah
is very beautiful. Down in Egypt she will probably
be in great demand, possibly by King Pharaoh himself.

You know that if you admit Sarah is your wife your life won't be worth a handful of that grain you're after. So you suggest to Sarah a convenient way out. She will pose as your sister. So your caravan arrives in Egypt, and just as you feared, the Egyptians lose no time in noticing the beautiful Sarah. Pharaoh himself takes her into his palace— to become one of his "harem." Being a gracious and sporting host, Pharaoh treats you royally because he believes you are Sarah's brother.

This little fiasco might have gone on indefinitely, but God intervenes. Plagues hit Pharaoh's palace (Gen. 12:17) and someone (Sarah herself?) tells Pharaoh just who his new "wife" really is.

Pharaoh isn't happy with the idea of dying from disease and he quickly informs you and Sarah to get out of town. He even escorts you to the border of Egypt to make sure that you are on your way as quickly as possible.

And so you return to Canaan—something less than a conquering hero. Although husband and wife had a different relationship in ancient times (for example, polygamy was quite common) you still have plenty of moments when you're not sure you can look Sarah in the eye. God's prediction about your being a great and famous man rings a bit hollow.

But back in Canaan life goes on (as it always does) and you and your nephew Lot both prosper. The "good times roll." Ironically, those good times bring up a knotty little problem—one that may test your faith and your character subtly but thoroughly.

The story is in Genesis 13. You seem to have it made. You have livestock, silver and gold. You and your nephew Lot have herds grazing in the lush valleys of Palestine near Bethel.

But trouble comes because there simply isn't room for your herds and Lot's. You see your herdsmen and the men working for your nephew Lot arguing over whose cattle will use which water hole. The situation is developing into something that is soon going to get beyond just talking and arguing.

You and Lot talk it over and it becomes clear that two isn't company. Two is a crowd. Somebody's going to have to find his grazing land somewhere else.

The choices are : the lush Jordan valley (which doesn't have room for both of you) and the rocky, less desirable hills of Canaan.

And so what will you suggest? God has told *you* that you will be the father of a great nation. After your little mistake in Egypt you seem to be on the right track and God is blessing you.

You are a very important person, not only in position but in God's plans. So what might you suggest to Lot?

Well, you have every legal right to claim the good grazing land on the basis of being older and entitled, according to the custom of your day, to first choice in everything. An easy way out, true, but while you might be within your rights you might not be too wise pushing this kind of argument. Lot may become angry and force a showdown that will end in bloodshed.

Besides, if you are a man chosen by God, you should have more going for you than custom and tradition.

Also, you've got to remember that Lot is your nephew, son of your dead brother, and in many ways he is your responsibility. To claim your rights as the eldest might be legal, but would it be loving or even ethical?

Well then, what about another viewpoint? You could say, "Look, Lot, I'm God's chosen man and need this land to carry out God's will." This is the old pseudospiritual argument. It is a nice way to rationalize and excuse yourself for taking the best land because you are under orders from God.

Justifying an act of self-interest for a spiritual reason is a sticky trap that can catch any follower of God. Perhaps that's the same trap you fell into in Egypt when you lied about who Sarah really was because you feared for your life.

Of course, you can always tell Lot that you are willing to nobly face the temptations of Sodom and Gomorrah, two swinging "red-light communities" down there in the lush Jordan valley. You could explain to Lot that you want to spare him the moral decisions that he might not be ready for at his tender age.

But Lot might question your motives. He might gaze upon the rich pastures of the Jordan valley and the bright lights of Sodom and Gomorrah and have good reason to wonder if you are really being noble. Lot was along when you were in Egypt. He watched you operate. He might not be so sure you are the big man you are cracked up to be.

And so, Abraham, what do you finally do? To find the answer turn to pp. 160-161 or Genesis 13. (But before stepping out of your role make a definite decision on just what *you* would have done if you had been Abraham.)

Granted, not too many Christians are having "rumbles over water rights" today, but all Christians do face situations in which they must ask themselves, "Should I stand up for my rights here?" Of course, the real problem is: "When is standing up for my rights the right thing to do and when is it simply selfishness?"

Think about it. Does this little incident from Abraham's life teach you that a believer in God should not "stand up for his rights"? Does Christianity really fit in with today's society? From the cradle most people are taught to compete, to hustle, to be first, to do their best, etc. The entire framework of society is built on the premise that you should do everything that you can to better and improve yourself. This secular approach to life brings up interesting questions for the Christian.

Does Christ urge His followers to be first, best, own the nicest clothes, sharpest car, etc.? For some direct quotes try Mark 9:33–37; Luke 16:1–13; Matt. 19:16–24.

God doesn't label material success off limits for Christians, but He does say "pursue with caution." It's just too easy to start using people to fan the flames of your love affair with things. It's such a short step from self-respect and pulling your own weight to manipulating people and (if necessary) trampling on them in order to get what you want.

LOVE PEOPLE

USe Things[1]

What's that? You say you don't manipulate or trample people? All right, that's possible. But what about "playing it safe"? You can live a very selfish life by simply refusing to get involved. Just be careful and mind your own business. Be sure to avoid . . .

The Disadvantages of Life

Watch the elevator doors . . . you might get pinched.

Hmmm . . . careful of the newspaper . . .

and that window!

Careful whenever you're watching something

or someone go by . . .

  AND PLEASE,

PLEASE DON'T POP THE BALLOON . . .

DON'T POP **MY** BALLOON.

Don't get too close to someone . . .

never know what might happen.

Everything might go up in smoke!

And if you're in a hurry,

don't get caught waiting.

And watch how things balance . . .

could fall right off the edge . . . catastrophe!

Careful. CARE-ful. Care-FUL.

People everywhere . . . EVERYWHERE . . . and you're

in the middle . . . in the middle of everyone.

Careful, they're watching you, looking at YOU.

They've got problems they want to give to YOU.

You know, competition, wars, prejudice, hatred . . .
oh, the disadvantages of life!
Escape if you can. You know . . . **LA LA LA**
your way through life.
But if you decide to stay around
and be part of the struggle for sanity,
you might not want to go it all on your own.
You may want some help from HIM.
(You know the One.)
He didn't create the problems on earth . . . uh, uh.
But He does have a "good cause" . . . you know,
peace on earth, good will to men.
It's a nice idea.[2]

Why not take a sheet of paper and ask yourself a
few personal questions about how selfish you really
are? Just how desirable is this free-swinging motto,
"Do your own thing"? Is that where it's really at?
How can you do your own thing and match it up
with the right thing? Life is one incident after another in which we choose between being selfish or
unselfish, between putting number one first or putting others first. As Glen Campbell put it, "I'll think
a little more of others and a little less of me." It's a
nice idea.

It's my move

Recent incidents in which I
"stood up for my rights" and was
selfish about it: _____

_____

This week I will trust God by
being unselfish enough to put
myself second and others first
in the following ways: _____

_____

_____

Let me be a little kinder...
verses that might remind me:
Matthew 16:24-26; Romans 14:13-23;
Philippians 2:1-11.

CHAPTER 3

DR. JEKYLL AND MR. HYDE?

Almost everyone has heard of Robert Louis Stevenson's *Dr. Jekyll and Mr. Hyde.*

The story came out of a dream that Stevenson had, actually a nightmare. From his horrifying yet fascinating dream, Stevenson concocted the tale of a man who was able to mix a potion that could separate his evil nature from his good nature. When he drank the potion the "good" Dr. Jekyll was replaced by the "bad" Mr. Hyde. When he drank the antidote, Mr. Hyde vanished and Dr. Jekyll reappeared.

But something went wrong. The nature of the evil Mr. Hyde grew stronger than the nature of the good Dr. Jekyll. At times Dr. Jekyll would change into Hyde without even drinking the potion. In his final rational moments the panic-stricken Dr. Jekyll wrote a letter that explained all his weird behavior (as well as murders that had occurred in the foggy London darkness). When friends burst through the door of his bedroom they found the letter but not the tall, well-proportioned body of Dr. Jekyll. Instead, there lay a dwarflike, hideously deformed Mr. Hyde, dead.

Stevenson's motivation for writing this story was more than a chance nightmare. He realized that all of us have two sides to our personalities—the good and the bad. Stevenson toyed with the idea of what would happen if a man could separate one from the other. He struck a horrifyingly true note when he pointed out that the evil can overcome the good if given the chance. When Mr. Hyde was turned loose he took over Dr. Jekyll's complete personality.

Stevenson's story of Jekyll and Hyde is a classic because it deals with a problem as old as man. But his idea really wasn't that original. The Bible is full of Jekyll-Hyde characters.

Paul knew something of the Jekyll-Hyde struggle. So did Peter and James and John . . . and all who have followed Christ for that matter. But perhaps the prize Scriptural example of the Dr. Jekyll-Mr. Hyde conflict is Jacob, son of Isaac, grandson of Abraham and twin brother of Esau.

If you want a little insight on your own Jekyll-Hyde hang-ups, why not become Jacob for the next few pages. Become the one known as the supplanter or to put it more candidly, the "schemer who took over."

As Jacob you can fight a real Jekyll-Hyde battle...

Bible scholars disagree on just when you lived but it was around the 18th century B.C. You were born "number two," clutching the heel of your twin brother Esau and this was the start of your Jekyll-Hyde battles. You wanted the inheritance—the birthright—that belonged to the firstborn according to your family's custom. The "birthright" meant that you would get a double share of the family's wealth (and Isaac your father wasn't exactly poor).

How you tricked your big brother out of the birthright, *plus* the official spiritual blessing by your father Isaac, is recorded in Genesis 25, 26, 27. It wasn't too much trouble for a bright lad like yourself. Esau was stupid and your father was blind and you got what you wanted (with a little help from your mother Rebekah who was on your side through it all).

But your scheming almost costs you your head because Esau wasn't a very "good sport" about your treachery. He threatens to kill you and your mother packs you off to see your Uncle Laban away up north in a spot called Haran. There you can be safe (and possibly find a wife and settle down) while Esau cools off.

And so you go north for your health and on the way you stop overnight at a spot called Bethel. There is no "Howard Johnson's" in sight, so you sleep on the ground with a stone for a pillow. And you have a strange dream. A ladder reaches to heaven with angels ascending and descending and the Lord stands at the top and says:

"I am Jehovah . . . the God of Abraham, and of your father Isaac. The ground you are lying on is yours! I will give it to you and to your descendants. For you will have descendants as many as dust! They will cover the land from east to west and from north to south; and all the nations of the earth will be blessed through you and your descendants. What's more, I am with you, and will protect you wherever you go, and will bring you back safely to this land; I will be with you constantly until I have finished giving you all I am promising" (Gen. 28:13–15, *Living Books of Moses*).

Shades of your grandfather Abraham! God makes you a direct promise that you will be an important part of His plans for His people. And what is your "noble response"? You say in so many words, "God, if you stick by me and give me what I want, then you shall indeed be my God. Why, I'll even *tithe!*" (See Gen. 28:2–22.)

What devotion! What spiritual insight! Yes, Jacob, you want to walk with God (your Dr. Jekyll side) but you also want to be sure to "get yours" (Mr. Hyde waiting in the wings).

You finally arrive at Uncle Laban's and your adventures there are well recorded in Genesis 29, 30 and 31. You meet your match in your uncle as far as schemers are concerned. You agree to work seven years (according to custom) so that you might marry his beautiful daughter Rachel, but he tricks you and gives you his homely daughter Leah (heavily veiled for the marriage ceremony of course). You're a good sport, though, and work seven more years to earn Rachel, and you marry her, too.

All in all, you spend twenty years in Haran, and through hard work (and natural shrewdness—see for example the ringed and spotted goats affair in Genesis 30) you become quite well-to-do. *Too* well-to-do to suit Laban and his sons. They grow quite cool toward you, and you can tell that they're not at all happy about all of your wealth. You decide (with some encouragement from God—Gen. 31:3) that it's time to get back to Canaan and your destiny as possessor of the family birthright. You haven't forgotten that promise God made you back at Bethel, either.

But you're not sure Laban wants you to leave. He stopped you once before and convinced you to stay because you were "so good for business." And besides, if he finds out you want to go he may decide a lot of your wealth will have to remain behind. So you wait till he's off on business and then you get your caravan on the road—your wives, children, servants, livestock, everything.

Laban comes home and finds you gone. He gets some men together and catches up with you. He

31

isn't happy about having his daughters and grand-children leave without getting to kiss them good-bye, but what is really rattling his cage is that it looks like you've stolen his family idols. (Laban, you see, is no follower of Yahweh. He has his own religion.) But you finally straighten things out and even make a peace treaty complete with a heap of rocks to mark the spot. And so you part friends (or at least cordial enemies—see Genesis 31).

But it seems that it's off the grill and into the coals. You send word on ahead to Esau that you're coming home. A message comes right back that he's riding to meet you with a welcoming commit-tee of 400 armed men. Things don't look too good. There you are with wives, children, livestock—a literal sitting duck waddling across the desert—and here comes Esau with 400 crack troops, a mobile fighting force.

You think fast, divide your herd, and send your party off in two directions. This way, if Esau at-tacks one group maybe the other will have a chance to escape.

Oh yes, you don't forget to pray. (The Jekyll-Hyde battle is still going on, isn't it?) While you've acted as if you can control your own destiny most of your life, there are always those moments when you do want to be a good guy. And of course a lot of those "would-be good-guy moments" come when you're in real trouble. (See Gen. 32:9–12.)

All right, you've prayed, and reminded God that the two of you have an agreement. But now what are you going to do? Esau and his men should be here by morning. Well, let's keep calm and consid-

er the possibilities. Obviously you could try to avoid the meeting. If Esau hasn't forgiven you after twenty years and he's out for blood, you are in a bad way, indeed. Perhaps delaying things until you are in a little better position to talk things over might make good sense.

On the other hand, though, you would only be delaying the inevitable. Besides, it's probably too late to get away now. Four hundred soldiers ride faster than herds and women and children can move—even when you've split the group in half.

Well then, what about setting up an ambush? Nobody could really blame you. Send word that you want to meet Esau in private because you're so emotional about the reunion, you're afraid you'll break down in front of a big crowd. Then kill Esau on the spot before he has a chance to get you.

Now that is really a Mr. Hyde kind of thought. But the Dr. Jekyll side of your personality isn't going to stand for this. You've already got plenty on your conscience about Esau and to add murder would only leave you with more guilt.

You never have been the violent type. A schemer who uses the letter of the law for your own ends . . . yes. A cold-blooded murderer??? No. So, you can't run from Esau and you won't kill him. Maybe you should think about using your best weapon— some oily double-talk to pacify Esau and to trick him into thinking that you really didn't give him such a bad deal after all. Twist things around, talk fast, and get the poor clod so confused that he will think *he's* the one who tricked *you* out of the birthright.

A very favorable solution perhaps, but the only question is, will Esau fall for it? After twenty years perhaps even *he* has gotten a little smarter.

Those are some of the options that you might have pondered on that night before your meeting with Esau. You and your party are camped by the river Jabbok and you go off by yourself to wrestle with the alternatives. To learn what you finally did do, turn to Genesis 31 and 32 or p. 161.

You wrestled with alternatives that night, all right, but you also wrestled with God. Scripture records that you went to the mat with "a man" and grappled with him all night. At one time you were getting the upper hand but finally, with a flick of his finger, your opponent put your hip out of joint and left you whipped and beaten (Gen. 32:25).

Yes, Jacob, you had to yield to God and realize that you are only a man and that you could not always be in control. You could not always win through shrewdness, strength, trickery or deceit.

Maybe that's the lesson from Jacob's life for believers in God today. Anyone who wants to follow God through a personal relationship to Jesus Christ realizes that he's a Jekyll and Hyde personality. (See Romans 7.) All of us have attitudes or habits that are more Hyde than Jekyll. Maybe that's why so many Christians sound so pious but remain so prejudiced. Maybe they don't want to wrestle with God about their temper, jealousy, insecurity complex and other hang-ups. But some do. One of them is a teen-ager by name of Scott Pinzon. One day his English teacher sprung a surprise essay test. So, he opened his paper with this poem . . .

TRY TO CATCH THE WIND

You try to love your neighborhood
And think you should
TRY
To do them good,
But you CAN'T, because
Your love is dwindlin'.

You see a Jew, and hate the sight
Because you're WHITE,
Which
Means you're RIGHT;
And you're both wounded
Because you won't let him in.

You see a black, and think he's a crook
You throw the book
At him
With one look,
And tryin' to LOVE is like
TRYIN' TO CATCH THE WIND.

Scott Pinzon closed his test paper by saying: "What can we do about this (prejudice)? It's natural to all humans, so there's not much to do.

"Yet everyone believes in something, a basic drive that keeps them going, whether it be themselves or the Bible or a religious philosophy. The only solution I can see is too difficult: everyone should live his faith not obnoxiously, but bravely and quietly. This can never be done by man alone, but he can at least try.

"And someday, if we work hard, we'll catch the wind—and be prejudiced against prejudice."

Scott added in a footnote that he believed he could live out his faith through ". . . a personal relationship with Jesus Christ."

Through LOVE one creates his own personality and helps others create theirs [1]

A personal relationship with Jesus Christ...now that just might be the key to helping Dr. Jekyll win his wrestling match with Mr. Hyde. If your relationship to Christ is truly "personal," you're willing to rap, yes, and even wrestle, with Him about your hopes, fears, plans and hang-ups.

Why not take a scrap of paper and wrestle with Him right now about one of your cherished hang-ups?

It could be prejudice, it could be temper, jealousy, selfishness, laziness. From Jacob you can learn that part of "keeping the faith" means being willing to admit it when you're wrong, being willing to confess that you've been looking out for number one while you have tried to become number one. But it's a funny thing. Becoming number one doesn't really make it—becoming God's man or woman does.

It's my move

Dr. Jekyll habits and attitudes
I want to develop—from
I Corinthians 13 and Galatians 5:
_____

_____

Mr. Hyde habits and attitudes I
want to get rid of: _____
_____

_____

This week I plan to do something
about one of my Mr. Hyde attitudes
by _____

_____

Some passages to help me with
the Jekyll-Hyde battle:
Romans 7:15-8:11; II Corinthians 12:9, 10;
Ephesians 3:16-21.

CHAPTER 4

REVENGE!

Have you ever thirsted for revenge?

Perhaps you're thirsting for it right now. A lot of us get revenge in subtle, clever ways. In fact a lot of us go to great lengths to get revenge.

Comedian Bill Cosby—with his uncanny understanding of the human condition—presents one
monologue in which he talks about revenge. It
seems that, as a small boy, Cosby planned one
snowy day to ambush his friend "Weird Harold"
with a light, fluffy snowball. (According to the
rules of the game only light, fluffy snowballs were
allowed. No slush balls—the icy, "gunky" kind—
were to be used.)

With Harold only three feet away, Cosby was
about to let fly when suddenly, "Whack!"—from an
unknown hiding place, someone let him have it
right on the side of the face with a full-fledged,
"extra gunky" slush ball and all of the juice and
goop ran down his stinging cheek, into his under-
wear!

Cosby turned and there was Junior Barnes,
laughing hilariously. In a blind rage, Cosby chased
his ambusher, but couldn't catch him. He finally sat
down in the snow and cried as the snowbank slow-
ly melted beneath him, soaking his four pairs of
corduroys.

From that day on, Cosby made plans to "get"
Junior Barnes. First, he made a snowball for Junior
Barnes and even inscribed his name on it. And then
he went looking for Junior Barnes but couldn't find
him. And so, Cosby had to be content to put his
snowball in the freezer and wait for an opportunity
to get his revenge.

Cosby waited, and he waited and he waited—
until July 12, his birthday. It was 104° in the shade
and there wasn't a snowball in sight.

He and Junior Barnes ("fast friends" by now)

41

are sitting on Cosby's front porch laughing and having the best of times. But the desire for revenge is still deep in Cosby's heart. He tells Junior he is going in the house to get them a bottle of orange pop (which they can drink together without even wiping off the top as true friends do). But instead of getting orange pop, he goes to the freezer where he expects to find the monogrammed snowball for Junior Barnes waiting in all of its icy splendor. Alas, Cosby's mother has thrown the snowball away. But this doesn't stop Cosby. He goes back out to the porch and gets his revenge with gusto . . .

He spits on Junior Barnes.[1]

All of us can remember times (perhaps quite recently) when we have gotten our revenge; when we have "spit" on someone who has done us dirt, made us look bad, defeated us, etc. To get revenge is one of the most natural of human traits. To strike back is an almost automatic reflex.

And yet somehow we know that there is something wrong with getting revenge. We feel deep inside that there is something a bit rotten about getting back at the other guy and making him pay for what he has done to us.

Scripture is full of stories in which men get revenge or at least they're tempted to do so. (About now you should be muttering, "Here it comes. Who does he want me to be *this* time?")

Well, if you've been turning to the back of the book to "find out what happened," you've figured out by now that these Old Testament characters are coming in chronological order. *So.....*

42

This time you're Joseph— the fresh kid who bugged his big brothers

Yes, Joseph, you're the favorite son of the Jekyll-Hyde schemer from chapter 3, Jacob.

But while you are your father's favorite you don't win any popularity contests with your eleven brothers. In fact, Joseph, you are something of a conceited punk and you lord it over your brothers with your claims of superiority until they get fed up and sell you as a slave to a passing caravan headed for Egypt (Genesis 37).

Once there, you become the servant of Potiphar, a big wheel in the Egyptian army. Things go well for awhile but you finally wind up in prison on a trumped-up morals charge.

It seems your master's wife keeps telling you, "Enough of this old morality nonsense. Let's live a little. We can have a brief but meaningful relationship while my husband is on his tour of duty." Finally, after you spurn her suggestions one too many times, she dashes out into the courtyard and nails you with the old "he tried to rape me" frame-up.

The charge sticks and it's to the dungeon for you (Genesis 39).

But while you don't know it, prison is just part of God's plans for you. While there, you interpret some strange dreams that some of your fellow prisoners have. One of these cellmates turns out to be Pharaoh's chief butler and you predict from his dream that he will be pardoned and returned to his job in Pharaoh's palace.

Sure enough, it happens on schedule, but does the butler put in a good word to the parole board for you? No, he forgets all about you for a couple of years, but then Pharaoh has a dream he can't figure out either—something about seven fat cows and seven lean cows coming up out of the Nile River and the lean cows eating the fat ones.

Pharaoh mentions his dream to his butler and *then* the butler remembers you, this fellow back in jail with the marvelous ability to interpret dreams —sort of a spiritual type with some kind of "pipeline straight to God."

The butler tells Pharaoh about you and Pharaoh calls you in. You interpret Pharaoh's dream and he is so impressed that he makes you ruler over all Egypt, second only to himself in power and authority.

You have plenty to do in your new job. The dream you interpreted for Pharaoh predicted seven prosperous years for Egypt to be followed by seven years of famine (Genesis 41).

And so your assignment is to get the people to stockpile their food during the seven good years so they're ready for the seven bad ones. It's no easy task to convince the people, but you do it anyway despite their grumbling about that big daddy bureaucrat who is forcing them to do stupid and unreasonable things with their annual harvest.

But they change their tune when the famine strikes. Egypt has plenty of grain—you've seen to that—but the rest of the world is in sore straits indeed.

You're going about your business of running the nation and distributing food to Egyptian citizens, as well as delegations from other countries, when you hear of a group that has come down from Canaan. You decide to give them a private audience, and what do you know! Bowing before you are ten of your big brothers—the very ones who sold you into slavery years before!

They don't recognize you—you're clean-shaven and dressed like an Egyptian and you don't look anything like a bearded Hebrew. And so here they are—at your mercy in more ways than one. If you've been nursing a grudge all these years it seems you've been handed a gold-plated opportunity to get revenge.

Well, what about it? Should these back-stabbing brothers who sold you into slavery go scot-free? Why not send them on their way and tell them they can buy no grain here because they are suspected spies and enemies of Egypt. You wouldn't have any trouble legally justifying this kind of action. As second in command to Pharaoh himself your word is law. In fact, just a few days ago you turned down some rascals you knew were enemies of your country.

Your brothers had their fun—
NOW IT'S YOUR TURN!

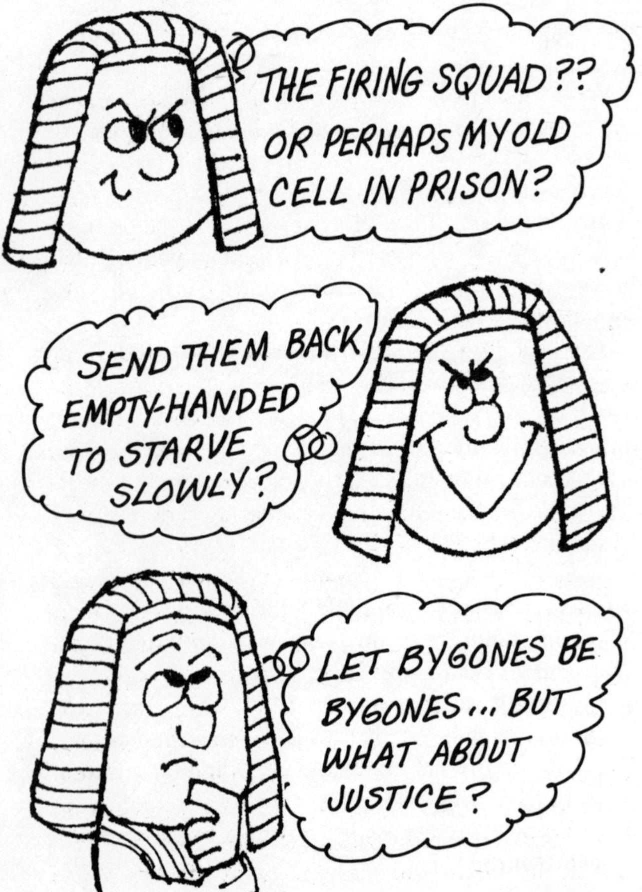

But why punish someone and not let them know why they're being punished? Of course, you could tell them who you really are and send them home empty-handed to your father. But then you would have the pleasant prospect of thinking about how your father would starve to death along with your brothers.

While you might not want to do anything as drastic as execute your brothers or let them starve, you might give serious consideration to letting them do a little stretch in prison. At least it would let your brothers know that they "couldn't get away with it." After all, won't it be phony to act as if nothing had happened? Won't it be phony to let your brothers get away with their crime?

Perhaps. But if the Bible is right and vengeance is really God's, not man's, then perhaps you should consider that the brothers have already paid dearly for their crime. Surely watching their father grieve after telling him a gross lie could not have been a pleasant experience. Surely they've borne the burden of guilt for twenty years. Probably a day hasn't gone by that they haven't wondered whatever really happened to you. In some ways perhaps it would have been easier for them had they really killed you and left you in that pit back there in the desert. Then at least they would have known what to feel guilty about.

Of course you could always just let bygones be bygones. Sell them their food and send them home with greetings to your father. That certainly would look noble but would justice be served?

For the fascinating and suspense-filled outcome

to this story you can turn to pp. 161-162, or read it for yourself in Genesis 37–45. But first make your own decision—honestly now. Nobody's looking. Had you been Joseph what would you have done? How do you balance forgiveness with seeing that "justice is served"?

Peter once asked Jesus how many times he should forgive his brother—seven times? Jesus replied, "Not seven times, but seventy times seven" (see Matt. 18:21,22). Was Jesus teaching Peter to neglect justice? Or was He trying to warn Peter about a subtle trap? That trap is to justify lack of forgiveness because you "want justice done."

There is a definite difference between justice and revenge. Rom. 12:19 sums it up: ". . . never avenge yourselves. . . . God . . . has said . . . He will repay those who deserve it" (*LNT*). Justice, then, is something that happens—through God's guidance and control. Revenge, however, is an attitude that eats at your insides because it encourages you to hate. And hatred always destroys—not only the one hated but the one doing the hating.

And so, the Christian who can forgive someone who has done him dirt is remembering to let God be God. It isn't always easy. In fact, for many of us, it is seldom easy. We try praying for the one who's done us wrong but there is no magic answer, no warm glow of "instant forgiveness." It seems that some of us have to pray a long time.

Perhaps you've felt like leveling with God and admitting that you're one of those who finds it hard to forgive . . . hard to love . . . .

For those who find it HARD to LOVE

My Lord,
I'm sure that you must realize by now that
you are asking me to do the impossible . . .
at least, it's impossible for me.
How can I love people the way that you demand,
forgetting about my own needs, to rescue them?
It's impossible.

And yet you say that people who do not love
do not know God. Don't I know you, God?
I want to know you.
I strive to pose a front,
a masquerade of love and concern for others,
for the ugly and the idiot.
But I know the sham I have created and so do you.

You show me all that Christ has done.
You say, "Look, there is love."
I see and say, "Amen." But after that I fall.
I need another step, I need a lift,
I need a power . . . I need you, God, within me.
I need some love genes driving me,
driving me to love, to forgive,
and to accept forgiveness from those I cannot love.

Please, God, may others who have loved show me
that power now to love the loveless and the dying,
to forgive the unforgivable and the lying,
before it is too late.
Bind me to Christ and make me over again.[2]

OUR LIVES

ARE SHAPED BY
THOSE WHO LOVE
(FORGIVE) US AND
BY THOSE WHO
REFUSE TO LOVE US[3]

God works with all of us at different rates of speed, according to what each of us can handle, but the important thing is that He does work with us if we allow Him to, and that is what faith is all about.

Carrying a grudge can be a heavy burden indeed. Why not think of some grudge you're carrying right now and see if you can't turn it over to God? At least try handing it over to Him to carry for awhile anyway.

Faith is, after all, surrendering to what you know is right. As you surrender to God in faith things get easier, and that includes being able to forgive. God and man are a team. Each has his own work to do. When man tries to take over from God that's when trouble starts. There's no more frightful or pitiful example of taking over from God than wanting to get revenge. There is no better example perhaps of letting God do His work in His way than being willing to forgive.

It's my move

○ I want to pray for _____
whom I haven't forgiven for
_____. I'm going

to begin thinking of _____
as a friend and not a creep.
I'm going to stop judging others
by not:

_____ being so critical
_____ being so touchy
○ _____ feeling so superior

I'm going to start letting
God be God by:

_____ being more forgiving
_____ being more positive,
accepting people the way they
are, not the way I'd like them to be.

To help me stay in a forgiving
mood: Matthew 5:39; Mark 11:25,26;
○ Luke 17:3,4; Ephesians 4:30-32;
Colossians 3:11-17.

CHAPTER 5

"Do I have what it takes?" is a question that all of us ask ourselves almost constantly.

It seems that as far back as we can remember we have been facing situations that demand that we come through, that we perform. In the everyday nitty-gritty of life, performance is truly a most important product.

"Get those grades."

"Score that touchdown."

"Be on time."

"Make that free throw with one second left . . ."

"Make that sale . . . solve that problem . . . get that raise . . ." the list goes on and on.

It's no wonder that the decade of the 1960s finally erupted into an inevitable reaction against the pressures of modern-day living. It seems that youth are fed up with the performance syndrome. Many of them are dropping out, copping out, and doing what they call "turning on."

Little wonder that one of the top rock tunes of the sixties was Simon & Garfunkel's "I Am a Rock." Simon & G describe the man who is a rock, an island, who builds walls to make a fortress deep and mighty that no one can penetrate.

The rock needs no friendship because friendship causes pain. Laughter and loving is what this rock disdains.

Don't talk of love to this rock because he's heard the word before. If he had never loved he would have never cried.

The rock is an island. He has his books and his poetry for protection and he hides in his room, safe in a "womb" of his own making.

The rock touches no one and no one touches him. He feels no pain . . . and he never cries.

"I Am a Rock" accurately describes the way many people feel these days. They'd like to get up at school, in church, at home—just about anywhere —and tell everyone, "Come on now. Anyone who asks me to remain calm and 'keep my cool' just doesn't understand my situation!"

It's funny how we decide we are unique. Nobody has faced *our* problems. Nobody has been under *our* kind of pressure. Don't give us that stuff about "back in the good old days." How can the wisdom of the past unsnarl our cybernetic tangle? Why, even the computers are confused.

What's that? You say the Bible has answers for *today?* Come now, life in Bible times was slow and tranquil—lying down in green pastures, being led by still waters. No freeways, no finals, no frustrations—just flower power.

But maybe the boys who lived back there in the Bible days might not agree. Noah, Abraham, Jacob and Joseph may not have known much about computers, but they knew plenty about fighting off the desire to cop out under pressure. Perhaps the bigger the man and the more faithful he is supposed to be, the more human he is under the glossy coat of varnish that sermons and Sunday school stories have painted on him over the years.

How about Moses? He was possibly the biggest name in the Old Testament, even more famous than Abraham. And like Abraham, Moses is often victim of overzealous press agents. Well-meaning teachers, preachers and parents put him on a pedestal of perfection. Their stories describe him as Superhero, who did it all as he obediently carried out God's orders without a hitch.

But what does Scripture actually say? It's amazing what you can find out by going right to the source, rather than settle for a "secondhand" Bible education.

So, try being Moses for a few pages. (You may decide that "I Am a Rock" could have been his theme song on more than one occasion.)

Did the mighty Moses ever get sweaty palms?

HALL OF FAME

According to the Bible, you begin life as a fugitive, Moses. It's a little tough to be on the run when you're only a few months old but it was necessary due to Pharaoh's "birth control program." You were born in Egypt about 350 to 400 years after Joseph lived.[1] It seems that when Jacob and the rest of Joseph's family went down to Egypt to escape the famine they just stayed on and multiplied into a huge nation. About the time you are born Pharaoh decides there are too many Hebrews for comfort and he decides to cut their population by killing all newborn Hebrew boys (Exodus 1).

How your mother saved your life by floating you in the Nile in a little basket, to be found and cared for by one of Pharaoh's daughters, is possibly the best-known story in the Old Testament (Exod. 2:1–10).

And so you grow to young manhood, enjoying the training and respectability of Egyptian royalty.

But you run afoul of the law again when you mix it up with an Egyptian guard who is working over a Hebrew slave. You kill the guard but word gets out. You have to flee the country or face a manslaughter charge.

You beat it into the Sinai desert—a good long way from Egypt—and settle down to a life of sheepherding in Midian. You even marry the boss' daughter and have kids. It seems that you've found happiness in the suburbs . . . except for one thing: God has other plans . . . for you and your people.

One day you're herding sheep near Mt. Sinai and suddenly a funny thing happens out there on the backside of the desert. A bush bursts into flame but refuses to burn up. Just keeps blazing away like a blowtorch with an unlimited supply of fuel. You move in for a closer look and a Voice tells you it's holy ground, that you'd better take off your shoes and listen up, because there's work for you to do back in Egypt.

What kind of work? Why, get your people out of Egypt, of course. Just go in there and tell Pharaoh, one of the mightiest kings in all the world, to let his Hebrew slaves go.

The Voice in the bush makes it plain that God is the one doing the talking, but this doesn't help you feel any better about what He's suggesting. Talk about pressure . . . talk about having to perform! You might as well be on "Mission Impossible." You drive up to the deserted phone booth, pick up the receiver and have the tape recording say: "Your mission, if you choose to accept it, is to go in and free all of the 'Iron Curtain' countries."

"Who, me?" is your brilliant response.

"Yes, you" comes back the reply.

So what are your options? Of course, you could be a good little boy and obey the Voice from the burning bush without any questions asked. Sure, go back to Egypt where your portrait is probably still featured on post office bulletin boards. And even if you're no longer one of the ten most wanted men in Egypt, just how impossible can things get? Going up against Pharaoh on your own will be like taking on the Kansas City Chiefs with a bunch of little old ladies in tennis shoes.

But then you can always turn the job down flat. Why not stay in Midian and the comfort of the suburban good life? You're safe enough, unless Pharaoh's FBI decides to range further afield after its fugitives. Saying "no thanks" seems logical, but you have to remember that while you were trained as an Egyptian in the queen's palace, your own Hebrew mother reared you. (Remember how she popped up down at the river bank when Pharaoh's daughter needed a wet nurse?) And so your heart has always belonged to the Hebrews and to Yahweh, the one true God of your native race. Now this very same God is talking to you out of a burning bush. One does not turn down cold a request by his one, true God, especially when it's coming out of a burning bush.

Don't forget either that you've spent many a night wondering about how your people are getting along under Pharaoh's whips. It's safe out here in the suburbs of Midian, true, but you certainly aren't free from your moments of guilt and anxiety.

So, while you probably won't automatically obey, you certainly aren't going to automatically refuse. You switch to plan B—offer some excuses to explain why you aren't capable of handling the job. Your first excuse is the tried and true "but I'm so humble" approach.

And God replies, "I will certainly be with you . . ." (See Exod. 3:10–12.)

A comforting thought, true, but it isn't quite enough to get you all turned on with the idea of going back into Egypt and making like Abraham Lincoln.

"They'll want to know who sent me," you point out.

"The sovereign God," is God's reply. "Just say, 'I Am has sent me!'" (Exod. 3:13,14 *Living Books of Moses*).

"But they won't believe me!" is your next protest.

This time God replies with action. The sheepherder's rod you are holding turns into a snake and then back into a rod. A miraculous phenomenon! Surely, Moses, you're impressed by now?

But your bag of excuses isn't quite empty. "Lord, I'm just not a good speaker. I never have been and I'm not now. My people are a tough audience. They're not going to listen to a stuttering farmer. They'll want a combination of John F. Kennedy, Billy Graham and Johnny Carson."

"Look," says the Voice. "Who do you think made you and your speech impediment? I know all about it and I'll take care of it. I'll give you the words to say when you need to say them."

"Lord, please send someone else."

"All right, I'll send along your brother Aaron. He's a good speaker and I will tell you what to tell him. I'll help you both."

"I'll think it over, Lord."

And so you head back home and decide to talk it over with your father-in-law, Jethro. What will you do? The answer is on p. 162, or see Exodus 4. Moses had to decide if he would face pressure or try to hide from it. Could he do what was asked of him and still feel that he was "being himself"?

That's the roughest part of it, trying to be yourself when other people are trying to make you into something else, or at least that's how it looks to you. You'd like to escape, get away from the rat race, the noise, yes, especially . . .

THE NOISE

The noise . . . the pressures,

the decisions . . . the **NOISE...**

QUIET!

A man screams for quiet.

A man wants sanity in the confusion.

A man wants release from the pressures.

They say Christ cares and wants to help . . .

No money-back guarantee you'll be free of noise,

confusion, pain, pressures, decisions . . . uh, uh.

He just says,

TRUST ME, MAN, TRUST ME.

"I've been through it all.

I understand, and I'll help you."

AND THERE'S HOPE IN THAT.[3]

There are two ways to react to pressure. You can become a rock, an island. You can refuse to open yourself to others and to life. You can think this will make pressure easier to bear, that it will keep a lot of pressure from ever reaching you in the first place. But rocks can't escape pressure. In fact, pressure can crack a rock, split it wide open. It happens all the time . . .

But there's another way to handle pressure. You can accept it. You can believe that Christ does care and that He does want to help. Maybe—just maybe—that's the way to develop a "real cool" not the phony uninvolved facade called "keeping your cool."

"You've got a lot to live . . ." according to one Pepsi commercial, and that idea is selling more than soft drinks. Human beings are not built to be only fortresses where they let no one else in. Human beings are made to love, to laugh, to cry . . . to have *feelings* (pain included).

Yes, it can get painful at times. People can chop you up . . . put you down . . . take advantage of you. . . .

‹ You can get depressed . . . angry . . . frustrated . . .

You can complain, "I just don't think I can handle this."

But God says, "I will be with you."

There *is* hope in that, if you'll answer, "OK . . . and I'm with *You*."

It's your move.

It's my move

I prefer being human to
being a rock because _____

_____

_____

Pressure points (problems, people)
for me are: _____

_____

_____

I believe Christ wants to help...
I'm trusting Him... especially with

_____

_____

Give me a real cool, Lord. Help me
remember: John 10:10;
II Corinthians 12:9, 10;
Philippians 4:6, 7.

CHAPTER 6

Afraid? WORRIED? WHO, ME??

Are you an optimist or a pessimist?
Is your glass half empty or half full?
Are you on the go or on the run?
A lot of people are on the run these days.
They're worried about the bomb, ICBMs, a cold
war with perpetual hot spots like Korea, Vietnam,

Laos, the Middle East. Then, there's pollution, over population and prediction of world famine.

Of course, if these "big issues" don't give you sleepless nights, there is always plenty of the nitty-gritty. What about tomorrow's finals, next week's rent or next month's payment on whatever it is you can't get along without.

No question about it, there's plenty to be afraid of, worried about—plenty of cause for concern. Everyone has fears, but the question is, "Do you handle your fears or do they handle you?"

One way to handle your fears is to be angry. Lash out . . . blow off steam . . . smoulder . . . this is an easy cover-up to make you think you are being "brave and courageous."

Of course, there's always the nonviolent approach to fear. Just go along with the crowd. Why sweat it? Play the percentages and be sure plenty of people are on your team.

The Bible reveals how various people reacted to fear. Some lashed out. Some went along with the crowd. Some, however, kept their cool. Because they had faith in God, they handled their fears instead of being handled by them.

What of Joshua, hero of the Battle of Jericho? The old Negro spiritual gives us a rather stereotyped picture. Joshua "fit de battle of Jericho and de walls come-a tumblin' down."

Just like that? It all seems a bit unreal. The fearless Joshua we sing about is hard to get in focus. But what if you could step into Joshua's uniform in less glamorous moments? You might get to know the everyday soldier and what made *him* tick.

As Joshua you're no "desk general."

GULP

Yes, Joshua, you were right there with Moses through it all. You toiled with the other Hebrew slaves in the Egyptian brickyards. You followed Moses out of Egypt through the Red Sea and into the wilderness. You came up through the ranks to become one of Moses' trusted generals.

As you and your fellow Israelites struggled together with Moses through the Sinai Peninsula toward the Promised Land, you ran across unfriendly types on the warpath. The Amalekites were one such group and you were picked as commanding general of Israelite forces in a big battle with them at a spot called Rephidim.

You and your men won the day but not without God's help. As long as Moses was on the hill above the battlefield, holding his staff high in the air over his head as a signal of trust in God, the battle went well. You had to be impressed with the strange power that came through an unlikely object such as a shepherd's staff and an unlikely procedure that had Moses standing up there on the hill looking ridiculous all day long. But you got the point. As long as that staff stayed up in the air, it signified that Moses and all the rest of you were trusting God and this was what really mattered. (See Exodus 17.)

But you had other experiences that built your faith and character. You would go with Moses to the Tent of Meeting—that spot outside the Israelite camp set aside for prayer to God. Moses would pray and then go back to camp. But you, so reads the Scripture, would not leave the tent until a later time. (See Exod. 33:11.)

Finally—after some two years of struggle and hardship in the desert—your entire band comes to the southern border of Canaan. Moses learns from God that he should send in men to spy out the land to see what it's like and how hard it will be to conquer. And so twelve spies are named and you are among them. Your assignment: look the place over. How many people? What kind of fortifications? What kind of military capabilities? What kind of crops? What kind of resources? You and the other eleven spies spend forty days gathering your information and then you return to the Israelite camp and meet with the whole crowd.

Talk about suspense. Talk about anticipation. Here are the Israelites on the verge of achieving their goal. Can it be done? Will it be worth it?

So first comes the positive side. You show them samples of fruit and other produce. Yes, it's a rich land and worth having, but then comes the shocker. Ten of the spies don't hem and haw around:

"We can't take the land of Canaan. The towns are all impregnable fortresses. The people are so big they make us look like grasshoppers." (See Num. 13:25–33.)

But you and one of the other spies (Caleb) aren't joining with the ten who claim Canaan is invincible. Caleb speaks up and says, "Let us go up at once and possess it . . . we are well able" (Num. 13:3, *Living Books of Moses*). But the other spies shout him down.

"No, we can't possibly do it. They're bigger and stronger and faster than we are. It would be suicide."

The crowd is stunned and then enraged. People weep with frustration. Cries go up, "It would have been better to die in Egypt than to die out here in the desert."

"Back to Egypt—it's our only chance."

"Let's choose a leader to take us back. Moses is washed up."

And so, Joshua, what have you been thinking all this time? Scripture doesn't really say. We might infer from your silence that you are on Caleb's side. On the other hand, you also may think the land is impregnable. People are screaming and carrying on all around you and the time has come for you to speak. What will you say?

Well, obviously you could agree with the majority report and admit that the Israelites are no match

On the GO - or on the RUN?

WHY ARGUE? THE CANAANITES _ARE_ TOO BIG FOR US.

IF I WANT TO REPLACE MOSES, NOW'S MY CHANCE

WHO NEEDS DEADWOOD! LET SOME GO BACK. WE'RE ON THE BORDERS OF THE PROMISED LAND — LOVE IT OR LEAVE IT!

for the gigantic warriors of Canaan. After all, the ten spies aren't lying. The men of Canaan are huge and muscular and they do live in heavily fortified towns.

Yes, these Canaanite boys are big and they are ready so why suggest an Israelite version of the "Charge of the Light Brigade"?

On the surface it looks like the sensible thing is to go along with the majority report. Being an optimist is one thing, but committing suicide is another.

Except for one thing.

The Israelites have no better chance against the giants of Canaan than they did against the Amalekites. But you had commanded the Israelite forces on the day they whipped the Amalekites. Why did they win? *Because God was with them.*

Apparently the other ten spies have forgotten the victory at Rephidim. All they see are invincible odds and a hopeless situation. Faith in God is fine, but the facts are too overwhelming. And perhaps you're wondering yourself, just how far can we push this idea of "have faith in God"? Just why should you buck the majority?

But pursue the idea of going along with the majority a bit further. They are looking for a new leader—to take them back to Egypt. If you have any ideas about becoming Number One, now is the chance. You are a respected military leader. All you have to do is agree with the other ten spies, then step forward and say, "Yes, I'm your man and I'll lead you to safety and save you from this madman Moses."

71

Now this is a real possibility, no doubt about it. It happens all the time. The trusted lieutenant decides that it would be more fun to be general. But are you willing to pay the price—to carry the burden of guilt that all traitors know so well?

Well, what about the other point of view? Why not forget the majority? If they want to be faithless and unbelieving, let them go back into the desert without a leader. Choose a select few from among the Israelites and go in and conquer the land commando style.

This is an intriguing possibility. Getting rid of a lot of deadwood would probably make the task easier.

For the final chapter in this spy drama, turn to pp. 163-164, or Num. 14:6–10. Joshua had to make the choice facing anyone who claims faith in God: "Shall I be practical about this? Shall I stand pat? Why try something that might fail? Or should I take a shot at it? Shall I see the possibilities instead of the problems?"

Have you ever thought about the possible connection between having the good sense to play it safe and simply being afraid? Not that you shouldn't practice common sense, but often "let's be sensible about this" is a neat cop-out that excuses you from trying. To not try is the safer, more sensible way to go. If you don't try, you can't fail.

Failure is never much fun. A young man named David wrote the following prayer. The subject is failure. Not much "rah-rah" here. No spiritual pat answers. David just empties his heart to God and tells Him how it is to have a perfect record—.000.

Did YOU ever FAIL, Lord?

No one pays any attention to me
or what I say, Lord.
　　I'm nobody, I guess.
I haven't done anything important
or made anything
or won anything.
No one listens when I talk,
no one asks my opinion.
　　I'm just there
　　like a window
　　or a chair.

I tried to build a boat once,
but it fell apart.
I tried to make the baseball team,
but I always threw past third base.
I wrote some articles
for our school paper,
but they didn't want them.
I even tried out for the school play,
but the other kids laughed
when I read my lines.
　　I seem to fail
　　at everything.

I don't try anymore
because I'm afraid to fail.
And no one likes to fail
all the time.

If only there was something I could do,
something I could shout about,
something I could make
that was my work,
only mine.
And people would say,
"David did that!"
And my parents would say,
"We're proud of you, son!"

But I can't do anything.
Everyone else is so much better
at everything
than I am.
The more I fail
the more it eats away at me
   until I feel weak inside.
   I feel like I'm nothing.

Lord,
the world seems full of heroes
and idols and important people.

Where are all the failures?
Where are they hiding?
Where are people like me?
Did you ever fail, Lord?
Did you?
Do you know how I feel?

Do you know what it's like
when everyone looks up at you and says:
"He's a failure."[1]

74

Hopefully things aren't quite as tough for you as they seem to be for David. He comes through as something less than "on the victory side." But the saddest thing about David's prayer is the line that reads: "I don't try anymore because I'm afraid to fail." To be afraid to try because you might fail is a paralyzing thing.

How about your own fears? How about your own failures? (Go ahead and admit a few—nobody's looking.) Ask yourself, "What disturbs me about this? Just what exactly is bugging me?"

Jesus taught many lessons about how to live and all of them centered on being willing to let go of things. Figure out why you get frustrated and why you have fears. Isn't it because you want something very badly? Isn't it because you are afraid you will lose your reputation or drop in social standing? Isn't your pride usually at stake?

If Christians really believe they are saved by grace and not by works, why do they put so much emphasis on success? Search the pages of Scripture and you find no teaching that says, "Christian, you have to be a success." But you find an awful lot of teaching that says, "Christian, I want you to try because you trust me." (For example, see the parable of the talents, Matt. 25:14–30; and the parable of the two sons, Matt. 21:28–31.)

There's a story about an SOS call coming into a Coast Guard station from a ship going down off the New England coast. A young seaman looked out at the roaring waves and said, "We can't go out—we'll never get back!" But the old captain said, "We have to go out! We don't have to come back."

FREEDOM
is, after all, the chance to do better²

The old captain may have been a bit melodramatic, but what he said may shed a little more light on this idea of "I gotta be successful." The truth of the matter is that you don't have to be successful. Not as far as God is concerned. God loves you with perfect love and perfect love is supposed to cast out fear. (See I John 4:18.)

Christians speak much of being free in Christ. There is a theological side to that. It means that you're free from the penalty of sin. But there should be a psychological side, too. You should be free to be yourself—honestly and openly. You know that within Christ's love you are even free to fail.

Then you can relax and once you're relaxed that phenomenon known so well by athletes will occur. You will do a better job. You will perform at your true potential and you will know far more success than ever before.

You won't bat a thousand. You will probably still lose more than you win, but *you will win your share*.

Freedom after all, is nothing else but a chance to do better and Christ came and died and rose again to give you that chance.

It's your move.

It's my move

The reason I'm afraid of
_____ is because
_____

_____

I have freedom to fail because
God accepts my failures as well
as my successes.
yes _____ No _____ Not sure _____
This week I will "risk failure"
by _____
_____

_____

I don't _have_ to succeed, but
I need faith to _try_. Verses
to help me keep trying:
I Thess. 5:16-18; I John 3:18-24;
I Cor. 9:24-27; I John 1:8,9.

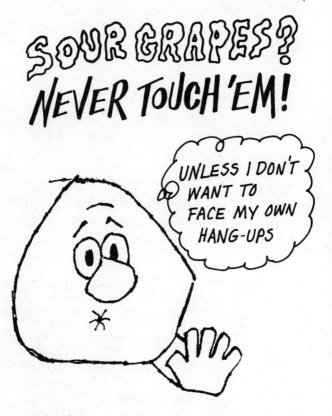

CHAPTER 7

"If only" is a favorite phrase that most people toss around.

"If only the weather hadn't turned bad."

"If only we hadn't gotten that penalty . . ."

"If only I had known."

"If only . . ." is a great way to rationalize your faults and hang-ups. The idea, of course, is that there was something you didn't know or couldn't help or didn't have, and it was because of *this* (not because of your failures or shortcomings) that things didn't go as well as they might have. But your ability is not in question, of course. Your wisdom and intelligence and charm and personality are all still intact. It's the little unknowns, those circumstances beyond your control, *they* are the cause of all the trouble.

In his best-selling book *Games People Play*, Eric Berne describes some 120 "psychological games" people play with each other in various relationships: child and parent, parent to child, husband to wife, employee to boss, etc. Two of the games Berne mentions are "see what you made me do" (SWYMD) and "you got me into this" (YGMIT). Anyone can play these games and everyone does, because we all need scapegoats to blame for our own mistakes.

Children learn the SWYMD game quickly from their parents. Little Johnny watches his father as Mother comes up and asks him, "Where can I find the pliers?" This interruption causes Father's chisel, paintbrush or whatever he has in his hand to slip, and he turns on Mother in a rage and says, "See what you made me do!"[1]

And then, of course, little brother turns around and plays the same game with his sister when she is walking nearby and he proceeds to break a toy or dish, etc. In little brother's mind big sister *must* have pushed him or bumped him. At any rate, her presence had *something* to do with his misfortune and so he cries: "See what you made me do!"

The "you got me into this" game is a little more subtle, but it goes nicely with "see what you made me do," according to Berne. For example, Mother goes out and buys an expensive dress. Father finally gets the bill, as he is desperately trying to balance a very tipsy checkbook.

"How can we pay these bills?" roars Father. "Here's a notice of an overdraft from the bank. *You got me into this.*" And of course Mother comes back with her version of *"see what you made me do"* by telling Father that because he had forbidden her to overdraw her account the only thing she could possibly do is buy the dress and not tell him.

SWYMD and YGMIT are just two games that are related to "If only . . ." thinking. (Or perhaps you might see "If only . . ." as a game all by itself.) When something doesn't go right, we've got to find a way out of it in order to keep our psychological balance. We find someone we can blame or at least try to suggest some reason for our difficulties. In most cases it never occurs to us that our difficulties really lie with ourselves.

Scripture is full of "If only . . ." incidents, and one of the most dramatic involves a judge and prophet named Samuel. The Israelite people turned on him because he was their leader and things weren't going too well. Try being Samuel for a few pages and you can play Biblical versions of

YGMIT and SWYMD...

Hey there, Samuel, how about a game of YGMIT?

GAMES ISRAELITES PLAY

You lived around 900 B.C., Samuel, some three hundred years after Joshua and Caleb eventually did lead the erring Israelites into the land of Canaan. The Israelites never completely conquered the land. Instead, they settled for coexistence with the Canaanites. Inevitably, intermarriage occurred and this was followed by apostasy and defection from the worship of Yahweh to the worship of Baal, chief of the Canaanite pagan gods.

The Book of Judges describes the sorry cycle of defeat and failure for the Israelites. They would slip into apostasy and idolatry, be oppressed by their pagan neighbors and then a "judge" would arrive on the scene to lead the Israelites out of trouble and back to God. These judges were part general, part governor, part priest. There were twelve judges in all and they included such well-known names as Gideon and Samson—mighty warriors who were flickering lights in the dark ages of early Israelite history as "every man did that which was right in his own eyes" (Judg. 21:25).

And so, Samuel, when you come on the scene, the Israelites are in another one of those in-again-out-again-Finegan situations. Their tormentors are the Philistines—a race of sea people who settled on the Mediterranean coast, but who frequently forge inland toward Israel to expand their territory. Because the Philistines have learned the secret of smelting iron (from the Hittites) they have a decided edge in battle with superior weapons and better equipment such as chariots, etc. While you can't help the Israelite armies with physical bravery or prowess, you do have a lot to teach them about turning back to God, and this is why they are able to thrash the Philistines soundly and push them back into their own territory. (See Samuel 7.)

Things look good for awhile, but then you grow old and the people become discouraged and restless once more. The Philistines are still lurking on your borders. Other nations are also military threats. Combined with pressure from without is pressure from within. It seems, Samuel, that while you have done a fairly good job of judging Israel, you dropped the ball as a parent. Your two sons, now administrative officers under your own appointment, are corrupt and the people know it.

Talk starts about the need for a king. It isn't the first time. When Gideon (one of the judges) had helped defeat the Midianites, people wanted to name him king, but he refused.

On the surface, getting a king seems like a good

idea. Up until the time of Joshua, the Israelites had been under what is called a "theocracy"—a government based on the rule of God through one definite leader. But after Joshua's death no single leader arose. That's what brought on the period of the judges, but no judge ever had the full backing of all the people, not even yourself.

Why didn't God raise up someone to unite the people then? Perhaps the answer lies in their attitude. At your headquarters outside of Ramah a group of spokesmen—elders from all 12 tribes—tell you how it is:

"You're an old man, Samuel, and while you've done a good job, your sons certainly aren't in line to succeed you because they are phonies and racketeers. We want a king—we want a real leader—someone who can straighten us out and put us on the right track."

And so the elders are playing games—their own version of "you got us into this." You are getting the old "If only . . ." line and the whole nation is handing it to you. They're telling you, "If only we had a king, Samuel. That's all we need. Find us one." (At least the Israelites are being religious enough to come to you, their priest and judge, to get a blessing on their idea.)

Now, you know God has planned a king for Israel, but you also know this isn't the time. The attitude of the people is far from one of obedience and trust in God. They are more interested in using the same political devices of the pagan nations around them.

Yet, if you refuse to find them their king it will

look as if you are protecting your own priestly interests. After all, you're top dog right now. You are the last of the judges as well as prophet and priest of the nation. You have the "establishment" to protect.

So, what should you do? As far as you know, God has named no king for Israel yet. The people are out of line in asking for one. You have every right to say no, and if they want to think you are protecting your own interests, that's their problem. Besides, you may be old and your sons may be corrupt, but you still have power. You might be able to face these elders down and still carry the day. They are a weak-kneed, bickering lot, anyway, and they probably couldn't get together on their own and select a king if they had to.

On the other hand, going along with the elders and giving the people their king is not a completely unattractive idea. Remember, you are an old man. You have fought and struggled and preached and pleaded and done everything you could with a stubborn and stiff-necked people. Why not simply say to yourself: "If I can't convert them I might as well join them"?

You know that naming a king won't solve the nation's problems, but the people are going to disregard God anyway, so you might as well go along with them.

Another tantalizing option is to resign. A lot of leaders resign when their position becomes untenable. Your conscience says don't select a king and yet the people are demanding one. If you resign, your conscience can be clear.

There are other variables. You might pull the old political stall game and avoid a *yes* or *no* answer. Why not establish a nominating committee to study what kind of king the country needs and who will be the best man. Then you can continue your efforts at religious and social reform and hope that public opinion might shift before you really have to come up with a king.

Whatever you decide to do, you certainly have to be tempted to do a little "If only . . ." thinking.

"If only my people hadn't been so hypocritical and apostate."

"If only the Philistines had decided to settle over in Egypt or some other place."

"If only we had the secret of iron smelting and could at least match the Philistines in fire power."

"If only my sons hadn't gone sour. I gave them everything."

"If only the elders had listened to my reform policies instead of going off on their own."

While you are a victim of the elders' version of "you got us into this," you can retaliate very easily. Just go off, name some clod king of the nation, let things really go to pot, and then turn around and say, "See what you made me do."

To see what you finally did do turn to p. 164, or I Samuel 8.

Being a follower of God doesn't prevent the "If onlys . . ." from crossing your mind. In fact, you are sometimes tempted to play the spiritual game called "If only God would . . ." or "God, you got me into this."

EVERYBODY WANTS TO BE SOMEBODY—

NOBODY WANTS TO grow![2]

But any follower of God—in 900 B.C. or the 1970s—knows that "If only . . ." thinking is a waste of time as well as childish and immature. The Christian knows that he is growing (if only by millimeters) when he can see that he is doing less "If only . . ." rationalizing and more of openly admitting his own weaknesses.

Why not take a scrap of paper and write down a few of your "If onlys . . ."? It won't exactly be fun, but it might be a real help. You might honestly face some of your real problems—for the first time.

Some people accuse Christians of living in a world of make-believe and not being realistic. Actually, the person who is trusting Christ is the most realistic of all. You have to be realistic to be a Christian, because you have to be realistic about sin in your life. You repent— ". . . turning from sin to God through faith in our Lord Jesus Christ" (Acts 20:21, *LNT*). And then you believe in Christ (Acts 16:31). You confess that He is your Lord and believe in your visceral regions (your heart) that He truly is God, that He actually rose again from the dead (Rom. 10:9,10).

Okay, you trust Christ for your salvation, but you have to go on from there. You're not perfect. Sin still presses in on you. The desire to excuse yourself with "If onlys" and games such as "see what you made me do" is ever present.

There are so many situations where you have to decide on looking something less than clever, smart, important or sharp. You may have to lose face for the good of the team. You may have to look as if you're being stubborn, square or even "unspiritual."

But you don't let circumstances and people dominate and dictate what you're going to do. You don't talk about "If only so and so hadn't done such and such . . ." You don't sit around muttering, "see what they made me do" and "If only he hadn't gotten me into this."

You simply say, "Guess it's my move, Lord. So, where do *we* go from here?"

It's my move

Some of the "If onlys..."
I've been using for quite a
while are: _____

_____

_____

Recently I've played "you got
me into this" and "see what
you made me do" with the
following people when I ...

_____

_____

_____

I don't want to play games.
Scripture to help me face my
own hang-ups: Proverbs 3:5,6;
Romans 6:13; 12:1, 2;
Ephesians 4:1-3; James 1:5-8.

CHAPTER 8

Out of the 1960s came a term that is now something of a cliche but it still describes a problem that has always been with us—and probably always will be:

Generation Gap.

As never before, adults were suddenly brought up short with the realization that they weren't communicating with youth. Youth helped them become aware of the situation with simple and direct means: riots, demonstrations, drugs, sexual experimentation and exploitation, and in general, a rebellious attitude that said: "We just don't buy your line of baloney anymore." Adult reaction was a mixture of befuddlement and outrage.

Some adults said: "Where did *we* go wrong?"

Other adults said: "How could *they* be so wrong?"

And a lot of youth said: "Wrong is a relative term. We think we are right."

And so the "gap" grinds on . . . although some people are tired of the term and stoutly maintain that there isn't any generation gap at all, that we should stop throwing this cliché around. True, not *all* youth and *all* over thirty adults are hopelessly at odds with no chance of understanding each other. In fact, one magazine went looking for a story in which it could quote teen-agers making *positive* remarks about adults. Some of the article's heartwarming comments (for older hearts):

"They stick to things more than kids do."

"They seem to have accepted themselves. They are real people."

"Adults are not hung up on the new morality like we are . . . older people really do something about changing things . . ."

"They've been through life and kicked around a lot and have learned to control their emotions . . . at that age you don't blow your cork or steam up."

"People over thirty have grown up so that they don't have to be 'in' anymore."[1]

Although teen-agers made the comments above, not all young people will agree. They've seen plenty of adults who have to be "in" and they prove it by the way they spend their money. They've seen plenty of adults who *are* blowing their corks, and they know plenty of adults who are *not* for real.

While some people on each side of the generation gap are willing to call a truce, plenty of others are still shooting it out. The battlegrounds are varied—clothes, hair, beards, the draft, religion, education, music. Possibly, the most crucial battleground is aims and goals. What is worth *having* and *doing?* The gap is there. No point in ignoring it or thinking it will go away.

Was the gap there in Bible days? Of course. For example, there is the story of a young prince who had to choose between loyalty to his father, the king, and what he felt was right.

Why not put yourself in this young man's place and wrestle a bit with a sticky situation where right and wrong are not clearly defined. Step back into Bible history and become Jonathan, son of Israel's first king—Saul. You are also best friend of one of the most famous men in the Bible—David.

Generation gap in Bible days? ask Jonathan

You are a young man when your father is named king of Israel. You join Saul's forces and play an important part in some of his outstanding victories early in his career (I Samuel 13,14). But then your father's shiny image begins to tarnish. Exactly how much he tells you about the "Amalekite affair" is hard to say. Perhaps he never does share with you the grim pronouncement by the old prophet, Samuel, that God has rejected him as king. (See I Samuel 15.)

But you stick with your father. You're there at his side in all of his battles, including that big donnybrook with the Philistines in which a skinny little nobody named David rockets to national fame on the strength of one well-aimed stone fired into the forehead of Goliath (I Samuel 17).[2]

Following David's victory over Goliath, he becomes an important man in Saul's forces and the two of you become fast friends. And so you watch the next events with mixed emotions. It seems that David gets too popular and too successful. Your father grows jealous and finally a little paranoiac. He becomes obsessed with the idea that he must kill David because, "David is out to get me."

Saul makes several attempts on David's life and even tells you and servants in the palace to try to kill him. You intercede for David and talk your father out of it—temporarily. But soon he's right back on David's trail again.

David can't figure out why Saul is out to get him and you're a little mixed up yourself. Your father's "now I'll kill him, now I guess I'll let him live" attitude makes it hard to predict just what he will do.

You meet David secretly and tell him you'll make one more effort to find out how Saul really feels. In a few days you'll return to the field where David is hiding and give him the word—good or bad.

You return home to the palace. Saul seems calm enough. A couple of days later he asks, "Where is David? Why isn't he coming to dinner?" You explain that David wanted to go down to Bethlehem to see his brothers and that is why he isn't coming to dine at the king's table.

Saul erupts once more. He calls you names and then lays it on you—and hard: "Don't you know as long as David lives your chances of becoming king are just about zero? We've got to find him and kill him."

"What's David done to deserve death?" you ask.

"Plunk!" Your father's spear terminates the conversation. He missed—this time. Angry and bewildered, you decide you had better get out of there.

Your father means business. David is a dead man if you don't warn him. On the other hand, if you do warn David and Saul finds out, you might wind up dead yourself.

It's one of those sticky situations with no easy answer. You could help Saul kill David because of loyalty to your father and yourself. After all, you and your father would like to have the kingship remain in your own tribe (Benjamin). The idea of being king certainly isn't unattractive. You've got a good military record, too. You've proved you are a brave and able leader. You don't have any Goliaths to your credit, but there's no question about your ability as a soldier and a leader of men. You

Decision at Generation Gap—

BE LOYAL TO DAVID OR MY FATHER?

IS "BEING BEST FRIENDS" WORTH GIVING UP THE THRONE?

WHY NOT REFUSE TO GET INVOLVED? — QUE SERA SERA. IF DAVID GETS KILLED, HIS BLOOD ISN'T ON MY HANDS.

MAYBE I'D BE DOING DAVID A FAVOR TO LET SAUL GET IT OVER WITH QUICK AND CLEAN!

have shown in the past that you are a take-charge kind of guy—like when you and your armor-bearer defeated an entire Philistine garrison at Michmash (I Samuel 14).

On the other hand, you could play it cool and say nothing. You could just fail to show up for your appointment with David. He might take the hint and try to make a getaway. Or he might think the coast is clear and come walking into a trap.

Either way, sooner or later, with all of his soldiers, spies and power, Saul will find David and kill him. If you stay out of it you won't have to worry too much about gruff old Samuel stepping in to block your rise to the throne. Yes, quiet uninvolvement might be the smartest strategy here after all.

Of course, you can always forget all this political ambition. Be the proverbial "good guy in the white helmet." David is your sworn friend—forever. Yes, warning David certainly seems to be the noble thing to do. But what about your father? He's not perfect, but he is still your father.

Then, too, for all you know you might be doing David a favor if you let him be killed quickly and cleanly. Why let him suffer as a fugitive, hunted like an animal? You're a man of war. You've seen men die and maybe the best way out for David is a quick and honorable death, battling against hopeless odds as one of Saul's execution squads cuts him down.

To learn what you finally did do, turn to p. 165, or read I Samuel 20. As you probably guessed, you do warn David, but what you do *afterward* makes the most interesting part of the story.

The way most lessons or sermons on Jonathan put it, *naturally* Jonathan would warn David because he would want to help his best friend get away. But who's to say what really went through Jonathan's mind? Who is to say what kind of battles he fought and what kind of wrestling match he had with his own conscience and his own pride and ambition? No matter how you slice it, when Jonathan warned David, he helped widen his own personal generation gap between himself and his father. He spurned his father's hopes of seeing his son carry on as king of Israel.

It seems that Jonathan and Saul couldn't agree on what was important and of real value. Maybe that is why young and old fail so often to hear one another. The adult establishment is usually blamed for not listening. As one teen-ager put it:

"Listening requires concentration. Concentration requires time. Some parents don't have the time; therefore, they don't REALLY listen to their children.

"Talking to a parent who wears a blank look on his face is distressing—like talking to a wall."[3]

Granted, plenty of parents are like a wall. They fail to listen; they misinterpret; they fly off the handle. But not all parents are like that. Perhaps some parents and more of the adult establishment than teen-agers might be willing to hope for would identify with the father on the next page . . .

... Irrelevant Dialogue[4]

Yes, can't both sides just try to talk?

Just how real and widespread the generation gap actually is can be debated. But what is hardly debatable is that the "gap flap" of the sixties and the seventies will have to produce a more honest and realistic approach to deciding between right and wrong, a new willingness on the part of parents and children to relate to one another openly with real respect.

That there has been a great deal of hypocrisy among those over thirty is without question. That some parents put down their teen-agers with no concern for how they feel is also true. That many adults are "out of it" as far as making the gospel relevant to today is painfully obvious.

Those under thirty have done a beautiful job of turning the searchlight of truth on the post-thirty hypocrites. Sooner or later, however, the under thirty generation will have to deal with the log in its own eye.

And perhaps bridging the generation gap will be up to younger people (younger in age *or* attitude) who are willing to change. Jonathan might be a good model to go by. Jonathan did what he knew was right, and he didn't worry too much about himself. He did warn David and helped him get away, but notice he didn't follow David into the hills and become an outlaw, too. He didn't sneak back to the palace and slip his father a knife in the ribs or a dose of poison in self-defense.

No, Jonathan went back, took the abuse and hatred that his father must have handed out and then he stuck with his father and tried to help him

There is an old Chinese saying
that each generation builds
a road for the next... The road
has been well built for us and
I believe it is up to us in
our generation to build our
road for the next generation[5]

John F. Kennedy

hold the kingdom together. And what did Jonathan get for his trouble? Death at the end of a Philistine sword—fighting to the last with his father in a battle in which they were hopelessly outnumbered (I Samuel 31).

Now, all this doesn't sound "too swift." Jonathan was a nice guy and he definitely finished last. He went around saying, "It's not whether I win or lose, it's how I play the game." And where did it all get him?

Sort of reminds you of Jesus, doesn't it? He was for the underdog and for doing the right thing and all that, and look how *He* wound up. But it sort of makes you wonder. Maybe there's more to this business of having faith in God than always coming out on top of the human heap.

Jonathan may have "disobeyed" his father, but he certainly didn't dishonor him. Perhaps Jonathan already knew something that Jesus would teach: "If you try to save your life, you will lose it, but if you lose it for the sake of others, you'll save it."

It's everybody's move.

It's my move

1. To be honest, there seems to be a generation gap between me and _____

2. I'm going to do something constructive about bridging that gap by:

___ trying to put myself in the other person's shoes.

___ accepting that other person even though we like different kinds of music, styles, etc.

___ being as honest with the other person, as both of us can stand.

___ trying to "hear" the other person, not just pretend I'm listening

Some reminders to keep me working on the bridge across the gap: Prov. 16:19; 29:23; Micah 6:8; Matt. 18:4; Rom. 12:9-21; I Cor. 13:4-7; Eph. 4:23; Phil. 2:4; I Peter 5:5.

CHAPTER 9

I'M WILLING TO LISTEN TO REASON!

UNLESS YOU DISAGREE WITH ME

Here's a little quiz for you:
1. What causes most arguments?
2. Does it really help to "win an argument"?
3. How can you avoid arguments?

Paul Tournier, one of the top psychiatrists of the 20th century, has written, "In all my life I can remember only one argument which really changed my mind."[1] Tournier observes that when two people argue, they seldom really communicate. Each defends what he believes "has got to be true." That the other person might be at least partially right doesn't seem possible.

Behind every argument is a basic characteristic found in most human beings: we speak and act according to our prejudices and our biases, how we have been programmed to think and act. Our pride stands between us and the other person.

Scripture records many examples of how pride brings suffering and disaster upon people and nations. Throughout her history Israel suffered as a nation because of pride. Sometimes the pride was in one of her leaders and sometimes it was in too many of her citizens. It caused arguments which often turned into battles and even wars.

Although Saul, first king of Israel, was something of a failure, the country went on to its Golden Age under its next two monarchs—David and Solomon. (See II Samuel, I Kings 1-11.)

A man of many gifts, David was particularly skilled as a general. He strengthened Israel's unity, established the capital in Jerusalem and expanded his country's territory.

David's son, Solomon, was gifted in business and administration. Through a combination of God-given wisdom and natural shrewdness he built tiny Israel into one of the richest and most respected nations of its time.

There is little doubt that you could learn much about pride and the sorry consequences of not being willing to listen to reason if you took the role of David or Solomon. But instead of being a VIP, why not play a "bit part" and be right in the middle of one of the most crucial incidents in Israel's history?

So, this time you're not David and you're not Solomon. Instead you are Solomon's son, Rehoboam.

Dear old Dad taught you all the tricks, Rehoboam

HOW TO WIN FRIENDS AND EXPAND YOUR KINGDOM
K. Solomon

When it came to making money, you had a master teacher. Your father was a sort of cross between J. P. Getty, H. L. Hunt and a computer. You also learned about political reality from Solomon. He divided the nation into twelve tax districts, with each district responsible for support of the kingdom one month each year. With this system Solomon was able to finance elaborate building and military programs.

But your father's real stock in trade was trade itself. He capitalized on Israel's unified control over vital trade routes between the "four corners of the Middle East"—Asia Minor, Egypt, Arabia and Mesopotamia. In other words, if a caravan were in Egypt and wanted to go to Asia Minor it had to go through Israel, and that meant it had to pay taxes to travel Israel's roads.

You were the typical son of the busy executive. As your father built Israel into a rich and prosperous nation, he became more and more involved in business contacts, treaties and commercial enterprises.

You learned about women from your father, too. He acquired many wives, not because of a sex drive that worked overtime, but because wives were good business investments. As your father would make a treaty with a neighboring nation, he would seal that treaty by marrying a daughter of that country's king.

And it was at home where you learned firsthand about Solomon's faith in God. Those treaty-making expeditions brought your father a great many pagan wives—700 to be exact. All of your father's great wisdom could not save him from compromising and capitulating in order to keep his harem happy.

So, your father soon found himself adding a few extra touches to the spiritual life of Israel. Not that Solomon abandoned worship of Jehovah. He just included a few things from the pagan religions of his many wives. Eventually he paid the penalty of having God reject him and break the covenant between them. (See I Kings 11:9–13.)

So you grew up, the son of a man who brought Israel fame, splendor and a new high in gross national product. And all the while Israel's moral and spiritual fiber suffered from dry rot. Your father was more interested in things than persons. He drove his people physically and financially to achieve his goals. Interestingly enough, there is little record of rebellion or discontent during your father's reign. Apparently, people were willing to put up with the high taxes and the work levies because they thought they were enjoying their "higher standard of living."

Of course, everyone wasn't deliriously happy. One of the malcontents was a man who would eventually become your mortal enemy—Jeroboam, a bright young executive type who had come up through the ranks of government service. He held high office in the tribe of Ephraim, a powerful group that pretty well controlled the northern part of Israel.

When Solomon heard that Jeroboam was talking rebellion and insurrection, he tried to have him removed from the picture. But the assassination attempt failed and Jeroboam decided a little trip to Egypt would be good for his health (I Kings 11:40).

Solomon finally dies, after an incredible forty-year reign that puts him down in the history books as one of the world's outstanding men. And you, Rehoboam, the next in line, are named to fill his shoes.

Will you be able to handle it? Will you be able to keep the restless northern natives happy? For openers you decide on a diplomatic move. You will go up to Shechem, the northern part of Israel, and be crowned king there. It's a formality, of course. You have already taken office in Jerusalem, but going through a public ceremony up in Shechem should have tremendous public relations value.

You will pay the people of the northern area tribute by coming to their town for a coronation.

But when you get there, guess who's waiting with his band of cronies. Yes, it's Jeroboam, with a seemingly reasonable request: "Solomon, your father, worked us pretty hard," says Jeroboam. "We're wondering if you will be willing to reduce the taxes and the voluntary labor assignments."

Jeroboam catches you off guard just a little bit, but you stall him with the typical political tactic: "Give me some time to think it over. I'll talk to you again in three days."

And so, you call in the advisory council (your "presidential cabinet") to get their views.

Older men in your cabinet advise you to go ahead and lower taxes and the work load. They tell you that if you "speak good words" on tax reform and less forced labor, you will have an obedient, happy and loyal nation over which to rule.

And then you turn to younger men in your council—some of whom you have grown up with. They do not agree.

"Show them who's boss," is their advice. "Do you want to look like a weakling? You've got to look strong—even stronger than your father was. Tell Jeroboam and the rest that you're not going to lower taxes, but you'll raise them; that you're not going to lessen the work load, but you'll increase it. Men like Jeroboam understand only one thing—power, and you'd better show plenty of it."

And so there you are, a new king, son of the mighty Solomon. For awhile it looked like you were stepping into a very nice setup, but now you

The natives are restless, Rehoboam...

GIVE IN AND LOWER TAXES? NICE KINGS FINISH LAST— OR DEAD!

MY FATHER DID WORK THEM PRETTY HARD. A TAX CUT COULD BE GOOD P.R.

MAYBE A FAT BUREAUCRAT JOB FOR JEROBOAM WOULD KEEP HIM HAPPY AND SOLVE THE WHOLE THING.

are not so sure. Dear old Dad never faced anything quite like this. But Daddy's gone and you've nobody to turn to but yourself.

Perhaps the old men are right. Your father did work the people hard. Perhaps now is the time to let them relax a bit and help them think about just how they're going to use all those buildings, fortifications, trading ships, roads and industry.

Furthermore, it's plain to see that up here in the North the natives are getting restless. To grant their request—at least in part—could buy you some time to do a little public relations work and reunite the country.

On the other hand, with a guy like Jeroboam around, your public relations work might be all in vain. The man is a real troublemaker. Maybe the best route is to put him and his friends down hard on this tax reform request. If you don't show real muscle now your whole kingdom can fall apart, and you may become just another statistic on the rolls of royal assassinations.

Also, if you grant this request for lower taxes and a smaller work load, you give Jeroboam every opportunity to become the grass roots hero who got King Rehoboam to back down.

There are possibilities in the "personal approach." Jeroboam seems to be a real problem here, so why not get rid of him? But your father tried that and missed. You might be wiser to get a man with this much ability and ambition on your side. Perhaps a fat government post with a high salary would turn the trick. If Jeroboam's main concern is really taxes, he certainly must have his price.

111

Yes, the argument grows hot and heavy between your senior and junior advisors and you're right in the middle. For how you finally respond, turn to pp. 165-166, or I Kings 12.

Rehoboam's decision changed the course of Israel's history, unfortunately for the worse. Ironically enough, he ignored one of the proverbs his own father wrote: "The fear of the Lord is instruction and wisdom and humility goes before honor." (See Prov. 15:33.) But then, that's not so surprising. Solomon himself ignored quite a few of his own proverbs.

Rehoboam's main concern was, "How can I get out of this and preserve my pride and prestige?" Apparently it never occurred to Rehoboam that he could trust in God—that he could have faith enough in God to give in for the good of his country.

Paul Tournier, the psychiatrist mentioned earlier, believes that getting tough is not a sign of strength, but of weakness. The strong person, says Tournier, can afford to give in because he doesn't have to win in order to keep his prestige. The weak person, however, gets desperate and then ornery because he has to assure himself that he is the boss.

Weak people, according to Tournier, "will argue against plain logic and will even stand against their interests, because they cannot stand being defeated."[2]

Perhaps this prayer—written by a young person —puts it pretty well for the Christian who wants to listen to reason but usually finds himself getting tough to cover his own weakness.

THEY'RE DIFFERENT, LORD

Why should I have anything to do
with people like that, Lord?
They're different.

If I'm honest with myself
I'm afraid of them,
and deep down inside I'm biased
like everyone else.

In my head I know
I should love everyone,
but it doesn't work that way.

I find myself
believing the bad things
about people who are different.
I listen to my feelings
instead of my brain,
to my fears
instead of my faith.
I can't seem to trust
people who don't think and live
the way I do.

I keep telling myself
I am more open-minded
than most people I know.
Surely I'm better than some people.
How can everyone be equally important
or valuable
or worthy of my concern?

But then you come along, Lord,
and claim that you died
and rose for everyone,
no matter what they are like.
Everyone is equally important
for you
and I suppose they should be for me.

But I can't see it.
Or rather I can see it,
but I can't feel it.
Give me the spirit
that makes me open
not only to accept people
but to receive them
the way I'd receive you, Lord.

I can't do it by myself,
I simply can't.[3]

Life is full of situations where you have to decide: am I strong enough to surrender or am I so weak I have to resist. Maybe you're facing one of those situations right now—a disagreement between you and someone in your family, a teacher, a friend, etc. Why not take a slip of paper and list your options. What will happen if you get tough and demand your own way? What will really happen if you give in and swallow your pride?

There are times, of course, when you shouldn't give in. There are times when you should stand for what is right. But the tricky part of it is that it's so easy to confuse standing up for what is right with your own weaknesses and pride.

114

No one is
a light unto
himself—not
even the SUN[4]

Of course, you are willing to listen to reason (if he will only agree with you). But some people won't agree with you—at least they won't agree with your hardheadedness. Having faith enough in God to pray seriously about your disagreements with parents, loved ones, or friends is no guarantee that the disagreements will dissolve. In fact, some disagreements may intensify. Even so, turning to God will be the first step toward solving the situation.

That was Solomon's problem. He got so busy with business deals and political machinery that he forgot to consult God. And in his first real test, Rehoboam also failed to consult God.

How about you? Think of all the arguments and trouble and needless frustration you could avoid if you talked to God first and planned to argue later. Chances are the arguments would never start!

It's my move

○ 1. I'm having an argument, disagreement, etc., with _____

_____

2. If I resist (get tough and demand my own way) this is what will probably happen:

_____

○ _____

3. If I surrender (give in) it might mean _____

_____

As Solomon said "before honor is humility" — Prov. 15:23. Some other reminders: Prov. 22:4;* 29:23;* Micah 6:8; Matt. 23:12; Rom. 12:3; ○ Phil. 2:13; I Peter 5:5, 6.

* Esp. good in "Living Psalms and Proverbs"

CHAPTER 10

Here's another little quiz you might try (if you feel brave enough). There are no "correct answers" and no final grade, but these questions might help you take a look at yourself (and sometimes that's dangerous).

Mark *A* for *agree* or *D* for *disagree* at the side of each statement.

1. If you really trust God and have strong faith, you won't be afraid in any situation.

2. If you know God well enough and have

enough faith in Him, you can know in every situation what He wants you to do.

3. Going to church will make your faith strong so that you can face opposition.

4. God will punish a person who doesn't stand up for Him when faced with opposing forces.

5. God expects too much of us when it comes to having faith in Him.

How did you do? The pat answers that are easy to toss around in order to look spiritual are: *agree* on the first four, *disagree* on the last one.

"Of course," if we trust God and have faith we won't be afraid.

"Of course," if we know God well enough we'll know what to do in any situation.

"Of course," going to church will make us strong enough to face opposition.

"Of course," God will punish a person who doesn't stand up for Him.

And "of course," God never expects too much of us in this matter of faith.

But the "of course" doesn't always pan out in real life. All of us have those times when opposition makes us run like a rabbit (or wish we could run). All of us feel guilty at times because we don't "stand up for Jesus" (and that guilt is fairly good evidence that we really do feel deep in our visceral regions that God *does* punish people who cop out on Him). Didn't Jesus say, "If anyone denies Me, I will deny him"? (See Matt. 10:33.) And all of us do have plenty of times when we honestly do feel God expects too much of us.

The answer is (of course) to have more faith.

That's a good answer. It's the "right answer," but it just isn't that simple. Anybody who is, or has been, encased in the package called the human skin understands this (even Jesus did in Gethsemane).

The Bible is full of people, great and small, who trusted God, but they still knew what it was like to be afraid and to cop out. Take for example Elijah, one of the big name prophets in the Old Testament. If you put yourself in Elijah's mantle for a few pages, you can learn what it's like to rise to the heights through faith, and then plunge to the depths through fear.

Sunday school quarterlies often picture you as something of a "superprophet," the fellow who bucked the pagan establishment of King Ahab and Queen Jezebel practically single-handed. You operated in the northern kingdom of Israel around 900 to 850 B.C. where Ahab was on the throne at the time. Like most of the monarchs who followed Jeroboam in ruling the Northern Kingdom, he was weak, corrupt and undedicated to God.

Filling Elijah's boots is no small order!

Ahab married Jezebel, the daughter of a pagan Phoenician king to the north. Her idea of fun and games was to kill every prophet of God she could find and to do everything she could to promote the worship of Baal. Ahab went along with her, and so did a lot of Israelite citizens, partly out of fear and partly because they weren't any more dedicated to Yahweh than Ahab was. It seemed practical to a lot of Israelites to switch to Baal worship because Baal was supposed to insure the fertility of the land and guarantee good crops.

But one day you walk right into Ahab's court, a rough, crude "Davy Crockett" type from the back country. You give Ahab the word and it isn't good. As God's prophet, you pronounce that there will be a drought in Israel until you give the word that rain can come again. This is pretty tough talk. You are bucking Baal himself, the god who supposedly can produce abundant rainfall, bumper crops and other goodies.

But your prophecy holds true despite many pagan prayer meetings beseeching Baal for rain. Three years go by and the famine is severe in Samaria, capital of the Northern Kingdom. You happen to run onto King Ahab himself and one of his servants—a fellow named Obadiah—who are out trying to find a little patch of grass to feed the king's mules. You and Ahab strike up a conversation that isn't exactly friendly. You challenge Ahab to bring his 450 prophets of Baal, plus 400 prophets of Asherah and meet you up on Mt. Carmel for a showdown.

You're riding high on the crest of a gigantic

wave of faith. In fact you're "in the curl and you're hanging ten." You are coming through like a real hero should. You have absolute confidence in God. You're willing to stand alone in your rags and match wits, prayers and even physical ability with 850 elegantly dressed professionals on the king's first team.

So the big day comes. The rules are simple. You will sacrifice a bull and so will the prophets of Baal. The god who answers by fire will really be *God*.

Baal's boys have first-ups. They dance, cut themselves and scream all morning and into the afternoon, but nothing happens. At one point you tease them a little and ask them where Baal is. On a trip? Asleep, perhaps, or at the restroom maybe?[1]

Finally, you decide this thing has gone far enough. You build your altar, put the dead bull on it and then have some assistants pour water all over the place. You even dig a trench around the altar and fill it with water.

With no possibility of hidden-match tricks, you pray to God. No joking now. Your prayer comes from deep inside, from out of a heart that desperately longs for your people to turn back to God: "Answer me, Yahweh, answer me, so that this people may know that you, Yahweh, are God, and are winning back their hearts" (I Kings 18:37, *Jerusalem Bible*).

That's all you need to say. The fire falls and the burnt offering is consumed, plus the wood, the stones, the dust, and even the water in the trench. The people all decide that God is pretty powerful after all, and Baal is a fake. There's a general uproar. Four hundred fifty prophets of Baal perish under your executioner's sword.[2]

And then, as if you have inside information from God Himself, you tell Ahab the drought is ending and that he'd better prepare for a real cloudburst. Sure enough, even though the day has started hot and cloudless as usual, the storm breaks and the rain pours down.

And so you are the man of the hour, *but . . .* When Jezebel hears what happened on Mt. Carmel, she issues an all-points bulletin and it's straight to the point: "Bring back Elijah, dead or alive, preferably dead, and in no less than 24 hours."

The news gets back to you—Elijah, the mighty hero of the Mt. Carmel Superbowl. What will you do? You've been riding the crest of that big wave of faith, but now it looks like you're going to wipe out. All those friends who were with you up there on Mt. Carmel seem to have dissolved into the shadows. You are left alone, deciding what to do.

You have your options. Why not send a message to Jezebel and tell her "Oh yeah? By God's power it is you who will be dead in 24 hours, not me." Then pray for God to strike her dead—the God-go-get-her approach.

This might work. Then again it might not. You might be presumptuous in thinking God would strike Jezebel dead just for your convenience.

Well, then just send word back to Jezebel that you're not afraid of anything because God will protect you—the it-can't-happen-to-me answer.

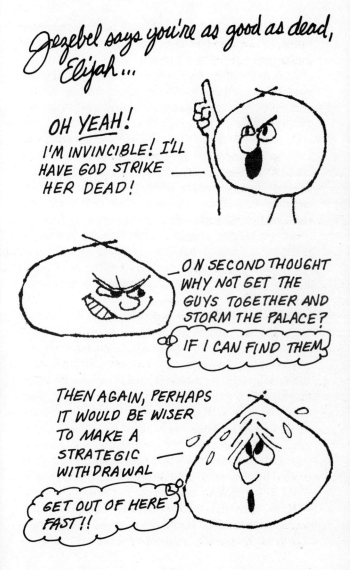

This sounds noble enough, but not too sensible. When you are pinned down by machine-gun fire in a foxhole, you don't get up and start walking around muttering, "God will protect me." When revenge-minded queens tell you you've got 24 hours to live, you don't brush it aside by saying, "God will handle it."

Why not go find all those fellows who helped you take care of the prophets of Baal up on Mt. Carmel? Organize a holy junta and storm the palace. Get Jezebel before she gets you—the wait-until-I-go-get-my-gang approach. This is a tempting idea. In fact, it looks like the logical thing to do. You really started things up there on the mountain when you executed the 450 prophets of Baal. So now you're going to have to finish things—*if* you can find that small army of supporters you think is available.

Well, there's always the old standby. Catch the first flight out—out of town, that is. This has its attraction, but it won't do too much for your image as Superprophet. You are the brave Elijah—the freedom fighter for Yahweh, the Fearless Fosdick of Israel, the Northern Kingdom. Besides, if you run, what will God do to you? Do cop-outs have any place in His kingdom?

Yes, Elijah, you must have had many thoughts when you heard Jezebel was out to get you. And what did you finally do? You decided that jogging would be good for your health and you jogged 80 miles south into the desert where Jezebel couldn't find you. For the full details, turn to pp. 166-167, or I Kings 19.

And so it seems that Elijah did cop out. The Bible contains no heroic chapter in which he storms Ahab's palace or fights to the death against overwhelming odds. No, Elijah turned tail and ran. Disillusioning as this may be, it does make Elijah a little easier to identify with. The Superprophet up there on Mt. Carmel, defying the enemy and calling down fire from heaven, is not so easy to feel next to. Oh yes, we sit in awe. We are impressed. We are inspired as Elijah does his thing and defeats all those pagan priests at odds of 850 to 1. But really *identify?* Really be like *that?* No, that's not for us. We're only mortal. Elijah is just out of our league in this ball game called "keep the faith on top of Mt. Carmel."

So, perhaps the real inspiration for the typical believer is found in the next installment of Elijah's story. He is hiding out in a cave on Mt. Horeb—deep in the Sinai desert. He has battle fatigue. He's discouraged. Elijah thinks only he is left to stand for God.

But while Elijah is down, he is not all the way out. He is still able to listen and he does hear the "still, small voice" of God asking him, "What are you doing here, Elijah? Get up and get going because I've got work for you to do."

And that gives Elijah hope. God's voice gives Elijah something to hang onto, something that helps him get up off the floor to try again. (See I Kings 19:9–18.)

It's when you're down, depressed, despondent, that the still, small voice of God can renew your faith and recharge your batteries.

It's a long way from Elijah's cave of despair in 900 B.C. to the rice paddies of Vietnam in the 1960s and '70s, but there are definite parallels. Things really haven't changed that much. The weapons are a little fancier. Things may be a bit more politically involved, but men are still having to fight and face death and despair. And they're still finding out that God cares—if they're willing to listen to His still, small voice.

Radio/TV personality John Rydgren captured the idea with this monologue dedicated to men fighting in Vietnam:

GROOVIN'
ON A SATURDAY NIGHT

Groovin' . . . on a Saturday night . . .

There's been a battle over here . . .
somebody's bleeding . . . his head is bandaged . . .
man, he's got pain,
but he's holding another man's head . . .
the other guy doesn't move . . . he's dead . . .
I know 'em both . . .

Groovin' on a Saturday night . . .
in a groovy swamp . . .
in groovy mud and water up to my neck . . .
Groovin' on a Saturday night . . . all dressed up.

Style? Jazzy . . . multi-colored . . .
to make me look like . . . a bush . . .
Groovin' on a Saturday night . . .

There's been a battle over here . . .
men have hurt men over here . . . killed men . . .
Groovin' on a Saturday night . . .

Groovin' on a Saturday night . . .
with groovy smells . . . jungle rot . . .
oil on my rifle mixed with burned powder . . .
and the dead . . . yeah . . .the dead . . .

Somebody's makin' coffee, I can smell that, too . . .
date bread . . . somebody sent it from home . . .

Groovin' on a Saturday night . . .

Bright lights on a Saturday night . . .
not flashing neons, baby . . . more like fireworks . . .
punctuated with flying lead
and the shrapnel's a groovy blast . . .
Groovin' on a Saturday night . . .

Some of us pray over here, in the battle . . .
the suffering, the brave, the afraid, the dying,
some of us pray . . .
they say God cares about a guy's pain . . .

They say that's what Christianity's all about,
you know . . .
Christ also suffering, dying, living again,
to bring hope and comfort to a guy
who believes it's TRUE . . .

God, I hope so . . .

Groovin' on a Saturday night . . .[3]

127

You may not be facing any showdowns with 850 pagan prophets. You may not be facing a Vietnam (on the other hand, maybe you are). But if you are serious at all about living the Christian life, you know it's painful to "grow in Christ." Like Elijah, you need the Holy Spirit of God to give you strength and courage you can't find in yourself. To grow as a Christian doesn't mean you struggle to become the kind of person you think God wants you to be. To grow as a Christian means that you surrender yourself to Christ.

Yes, you've heard that one about "surrender" before. Sounds easier read than done. But behind that pat cliché is a basic idea. When you believe in Jesus and take Him as personal Saviour you simply don't add Him onto your other "positive achievements." Jesus Christ isn't some kind of spiritual vitamin supplement for anemic moral character.

Being a Christian isn't a matter of working on your temper or conquering that desire to gossip. Those are good projects, but you can work on them without being a Christian.

To be a Christian is to become a "new creation" in God's sight. You do this through Jesus Christ. Jesus made it perfectly clear that with Him it's all or nothing. He is the way, the truth and the life (see John 14:6). The "work" God wants the Christian to do is to believe in Christ and trust Him (John 6:27). God takes care of the rest.

Why not just think about that? Quit dwelling on your problems, your frustrations, your complaints, your gripes. Just chew on one idea: "God cares about me. He'll never leave me or give up on me."

NO CONDITION IS PERMANENT

AFRICAN PROVERB

The idea is to get personal with Christ. You can't surrender to a bag of rules or a set of doctrines. You surrender to a *Person*. From that Person you get strength, love, purpose, a reason for living.

The Africans have a motto: "No condition is permanent." That's more than true for the Christian—especially when he's down and depressed. Then, if he has ears to hear, he can listen to the still, small voice of God saying in one way or another, "It's your move."

It's my move

1. OK, Lord, I admit I copped out
when _____

2. Lord, it seems to me you do expect
too much of me sometimes, but I'm
willing to try again in regard to
_____

3. Lord, I'm going to get together
with _____, who I know is
discouraged, and share the help
I've gotten from realizing that
you care about us and never
give up on us.

Some reminders that you care:
Psalm 91; Isaiah 41:10 Matt. 11:28-30;
Romans 8:35-39; II Corinthians 1:3, 4;*
II Timothy 4:18*

* Esp. good in "Living New Testament"

CHAPTER 11

CERTAINLY, I HAVE CONVICTIONS!

Who really determines the way you live? That is, who influences you the most concerning your behavior, the clothes you wear, the kind of person you are? To put it still another way, who do you most want to please? Take a look at the following list and number the various choices in their order of importance as far as *your* life is concerned. Be honest, now. After all, nobody's looking—but God.

131

And if He isn't really your first choice, He knows it anyway, doesn't He?

Close friends——

Anyone who convinces me——

Myself——

Parents——

No one——

God——

Other influences (try to be specific)——

Now, if you wanted to fake it on a little quiz like this there would be no problem. Obviously, for the "good church-going Christian" the most important influence on his behavior and life style is supposed to be God. But if you were feeling painfully honest when you checked this off you might at least have said, "Sometimes God, sometimes myself, and sometimes others. Depends on the situation."

Now it's not that you aren't *trying* to love God and worship only Him. But being human and all, it's hard sometimes to bring God in on your decisions. While it sounds spiritual to say, "I want to please God the most," the truth of the matter is that most of us are greatly influenced by "what will others think?" When the various pressures close in from your peer group, from your family, from your friends (and your enemies), it's not always easy to match what you do with what you say you'd like to do.

Plenty of Bible characters felt the kind of pinch that comes when you have to choose between pleasing God and "people pressure." Perhaps the most pressured of them all was Jeremiah, one of the major prophets of the Old Testament. Suppose you wear Jeremiah's "yoke of woe" for a few pages. It won't be a pleasant experience, but it might give you some clues about standing up for your convictions under pressure.

Jeremiah's yoke of woe may get pretty heavy...

It seems that God calls you to be a prophet at age 20 (Jer. 1:5).[1] You respond with about as much enthusiasm as someone who gets greetings from the local draft board.

You tell God you are too young, that older men are looked to for wisdom. But God doesn't listen. He tells you your age doesn't matter, that He will put His words in your mouth.

It's around 627 B.C. Your assignment is to prophesy to the Southern Kingdom where Josiah is king of Judah at the time. The Northern Kingdom (Israel) is already gone—buried under the onslaught of Assyria almost 100 years ago.

There is a three-way battle going on for first

place among the "big three": Assyria, Babylon and Egypt. In fact, even with King Josiah on the throne, Judah is already under a loose type of Assyrian rule. The only reason she hasn't been taken over completely is that the Assyrians are too busy with bigger fish to fight—Babylon and Egypt.

While most kings of Israel and Judah were apostate, weak and ineffective, Josiah is one of the few good ones. He tries to get a reform going. He asks the people to repent, clean up their lives and turn back to God.

But Josiah's reform movement isn't enough in your eyes. As far as you're concerned, Judah is doomed because of her apostasy.

Yes, Jeremiah, you are a strange one. You hate what you're doing. You even curse the day you were born (Jer. 20:14–18). Yet, you're so sure that God is with you that you keep right on going. You tell people the truth and they beat you, ridicule you, make life a literal hell.

And your prophecies come true. In 605 B.C. the Babylonians defeat the Egyptians in a big battle at a place called Carchemish, northeast of Judah in western Assyria. King Nebuchadnezzar leads his forces in pursuit of the Egyptians as they flee south through Canaan. In the process, Nebuchadnezzar's forces sweep through the Southern Kingdom of Judah and conquer it also.

Many of your fellow citizens are deported to Babylon and the year 605 B.C. marks the beginning of the seventy-year period of captivity that you have predicted. (See Jer. 25:11.)

King Jehoiachin, Josiah's successor, is taken captive to Babylon and Mattaniah, Jehoiachin's uncle, is made a puppet king of Judah by the Babylonians, who give him the new name of Zedekiah. (See II Kings 24:17.)

About this time, with Zedekiah on the throne and the Babylonians in charge, you will face perhaps the major crisis and test of your life.

It all comes about at King Zedekiah's court. The priests and many citizens are present. Up steps Hananiah, one of the "diploma factory prophets" of the day who got his training in a local school. You never went to such a school—you got your prophetic credentials from God Himself.

Hananiah tells the whole crowd: "Yahweh, the God of Israel, says this, 'I have broken the yoke of the king of Babylon. In two years' time I will bring back all the vessels of the Temple of Yahweh. . . . I will also bring back Jeconiah son of Jehoiakim, king of Judah, and all the exiles of Judah who have gone to Babylon—it is Yahweh who speaks'" (Jer. 28:3,4, *Jerusalem Bible*).

A murmur of approval goes through the crowd. "Freedom soon" is just what they hoped to hear. But now they're all turning and looking at you. You can just about read their minds. What will you say? You've always been the prophet of doom up till now. In fact, you've taken to wearing a wooden yoke, like the kind used to hitch up oxen, to symbolize the bondage caused by Judah's sin.

You know Hananiah is lying. According to what God has told you (Jeremiah 27), the Israelites are supposed to serve the king of Babylon until God pronounces otherwise. If they do not, the Babylon-

The people are waiting for your answer, Jeremiah...

HANANIAH IS LYING, AND I OUGHT TO CALL HIM DOWN— EVEN IF IT MEANS ANOTHER BEATING!

BUT I'M TIRED OF GETTING BEATEN UP. MAYBE —JUST ONCE— I'LL GO ALONG WITH THE POPULAR POINT OF VIEW...

EVEN BETTER—WHY NOT SAY I GAVE HANANIAH HIS IDEAS? I COULD STEAL HIS THUNDER AND BE THE REAL HERO!

ian soldiers will come back, crush the puppet king of Judah, sack Jerusalem and carry still more people into captivity. Hananiah is simply trying to score points with a popular prophecy. This prophet-come-lately needs to have his ears pinned back, and you're just the fellow who can do it.

You should probably come on strong as usual. Call Hananiah a liar and tell all the people they are as good as deported to Babylon unless they recognize that the yoke you are wearing is no joke—that it is a sign that they must submit to Babylonian rule as a punishment for their lack of faith. To disagree with Hananiah will probably cost you another beating, but it might be worth it.

Or will it? You've been beaten so often already. You're dedicated, but no masochist. It certainly is tempting to go along with Hananiah. Say that you believe he's right. Let him have the glory. In the end he will be the fall guy. He will be the one who takes the beatings and the ridicule. If you do go along, though, people might call you a cop-out. They hate you and despise you, but some of them at least respect you for a consistent stand.

There is a still more attractive route. Pick up what Hananiah has said and amplify on it. Steal his thunder, so to speak. Make it look as though you gave him the idea in the first place. Be the hero instead of the goat for a change.

Very tempting, yes, but could you really pull it off? You know Hananiah's prophecy is phony. Eventually, the people will find this out when Babylon comes marching in. Then there's that little matter of getting along with God and that fire in your bones. Things have been rough up till now, but one thing you haven't had to carry around is a guilty conscience.

To find out just what you did do, turn to pp. 167-168, or Jeremiah 28. But don't just get the right answer and let it go at that. Maybe that's why there isn't much commitment in the church today. We take a look at the Bible's answers and "let it go at that."

Okay, suppose you're not willing to just let it go at that, but you still wonder, "just what can I learn from Jeremiah to use in my own life?" Granted, he's not easy to identify with. Jeremiah was a unique man, singled out by God for a special assignment. But what you might learn from Jeremiah is the difference between having faith in God and *having faith in your faith* in God.

There is a definite difference between the two. To have faith in your faith might mean that you trust in what you have conceived and constructed. Or, to have faith in your faith could mean that you are trusting in what you have been handed by others, such as a carefully polished package called "our Christian faith and heritage."

To have faith in God, on the other hand, is to trust Someone far beyond yourself—a real Person, not just an idea, a collection of doctrines or a theological system.

From Earnest Larsen's book, *Good Old Plastic Jesus,* come some thoughts that might help you sort out the difference between having faith in God or having faith in your faith (the system, the rule book, the traditions).

Don't Just DO things
BECOME SOMEONE!

So many things:
faith . . . religion . . . responsibility.

Yet, only one thing: YOU.

You with your problems . . . with your aches.
Aches with no names.
Sometimes from too much joy . . .
sometimes too much fear, all of it—YOU.

"Who can separate his faith from his actions,
his belief from his occupations . . ."

God is not on another planet.
Religion is not just "things you do."
It is seeing God as a Person . . .
Becoming ONE with that GOD.

Forget excuses. Don't run and hide.
Just stand, LOOK.

Is God a Plastic Jesus?
Are you satisfied with Him?

The price is high . . .
are you willing to meet the challenge?

Not doing things—but BECOMING a SOMEONE.[2]

YOU BETTER NOT COMPROMISE YOURSELF— IT'S ALL YOU GOT. [3]

Folk singer Janis Joplin is credited with saying: "You better not compromise yourself . . . it's all you got." An interesting thought, but somehow it doesn't sound quite Biblical. After all, the Christian has more than himself—he has Christ and his faith. *But,* is that faith in God or faith in the system and saying the right thing? When you get right down to the nitty-gritty, what you are *is* really all you've got.

For example, perhaps what you are is a product of church organization, ecclesiastical machinery. You may be a spiritual parrot who repeats the catch phrases and slogans that are acceptable religionese. If so, you will seldom worry about compromising yourself, because what you are isn't that important to you.

But just suppose that while you're a long way from perfect you still know—deep inside—that God is more than a catch phrase or a slogan. God is more than a divine idea or a spiritual system for success. You want to be able to say, "What I am is the result of Jesus Christ. What I am is someone

140

who wants the Holy Spirit to guide and direct my life. I want a real friendship with Christ—where I can talk to Him like a personal friend."

If you decide to become what God (not what your family, friends or even that special somebody) wants you to be, it becomes a lot harder to compromise your convictions. In fact, you won't want to compromise yourself because you know that what you are is something you don't dare lose.

But "convictions" is sort of general. Maybe you need some specifics:

How about ethics—how you treat others? We all agree that loving people and using things is a lot better than using people and loving things, but do we live that way? Sexual hanky-panky, drugs, booze, questionable entertainment, etc., are all a question of ethics.

How you treat others depends at least in part on what you think of yourself. The Bible is loaded with specifics on respecting others because you respect yourself. For openers see I Corinthians 6, Romans 14, Matthew 5, 6 and 7, I Corinthians 13.

And what about the race question? Are you searching for an answer, or just hoping all the problems will be bussed away or bought off?

It seems natural for man to feel prejudice and hatred for those who aren't his own kind or color. But God isn't satisfied with leaving us in our "natural" state. For details see the familiar parable of the Good Samaritan, Luke 10:25–37, and what Peter had to learn about his own racist hang-ups in Acts 10 and 11.

A perennial problem area concerning Christian

141

convictions is witnessing. Many of us would like to say something, but since we aren't really the buttonholer type, we wind up among the great Christian silent majority. For a little different slant on the subject try John 15:1–17. There isn't much talk about witnessing, but Christ does mention bearing fruit.

"It is the man who shares my life and whose life I share who proves fruitful," says Christ in John 15:5 (Phillips).

If you share your life with Christ, you'll have something to share with others. You may not ever get too articulate about it. You may always be afraid to some degree, but as you learn to share your life with Christ, it will begin to show. Then, your verbal witness will get a better hearing.

To share your life with Christ—this is the giant issue. This is what Paul talks about in Philippians 3 and 4. It is what James means in James 2 and 3. It is what Peter is talking about in I Peter 2. And it is John's basic subject in his entire letter of I John— five chapters that can be read easily in half an hour.

Yes, there are many passages in which you can find plenty of support for sagging convictions. And there are many things you can do when it comes to "not compromising yourself." But it helps to remember that what you are is really all you've got. To have faith in your faith leaves you feeling dissatisfied, insecure and frustrated. To have faith in God through Jesus Christ, to share your life with Him, is to know that what you are is not only all you've got, but *He is all you need.*

It's my move

Lord, I've been compromising myself when it comes to _____

_____ and this is what I'm going to do about it: _____

_____

What I am is all I've got. Lord, help me become *someone* not just *do things.*

Scripture to help me:

I Corinthians 6 ; Romans 14; Matthew 5, 6, 7; I Corinthians 13; John 15:1-11; Philippians 3 and 4; James 2 and 3; I Peter 2; I John 1-5.

Memo: Need to get a "Living New Testament" or a Phillips translation to get the most out of these passages.

CHAPTER 12

AMEN! I WANT TO DO GOD'S WILL!

UNLESS IT UPSETS MY PLANS

"I'll be there, Lord willing."

Christians do a lot of talking about being sure they are in God's will. We've all heard the people who say they'll be at the game, the party, church or back to work Monday, "the Lord willing."

Now it's possible that some people really mean it when they say "the Lord willing." The phrase is Biblical. James reproves his readers for making their plans with no thought of God. He reminds them that their lives are as uncertain as the morning fog. Now you see it, but soon it is gone. According to James, what we ought to say is, "If the

Lord wants us to, we shall live and do this or that" (James 4:15, *Living New Testament*).

"If the Lord wants us to . . ." that's the key phrase. Sometimes what you're doing or plan to do is so far out of line with the plain teaching of Scripture, you *know* God doesn't want you to do it. Other times, however, it's a real toss-up. Circumstances, opinions of others, even your own training and knowledge, all make it difficult to decide just what God wants you to do.

The pages of Bible history are covered with men and women who have pondered, obeyed or ignored God's will for their lives. One thing is sure. God does have a plan for His people. He is interested in what they do, but He always gives them a choice. There is no better example than the Israelites. Again and again they would claim they had faith in Him and again and again they would go off on their own and turn their backs on God.

The Israelite attitude of unbelief finally brought complete disaster. Jeremiah's doleful prophecies (see chapter 11) did come true. The Southern Kingdom of Judah suffered the same fate as the Northern Kingdom of Israel. Jerusalem fell to the Babylonians and the Israelites were marched into captivity.

The Babylonians deported their victims for a good reason. They wanted to absorb them into their own society rather than allow them to remain together as an occupied nation still able to think about revolt and freedom. And so, the Israelites remained under Babylonian rule for some fifty years, until 539 B.C. Then Persia moved in and conquered

Babylon just as Daniel dramatically predicted when he interpreted the handwriting on the wall for King Belshazzar (see Daniel 5).

Not long after, King Cyrus of Persia decreed that all captives in Babylon—Jews and citizens of other nations too—could return to their native lands. But this time there was no wholesale exodus as there had been under Moses when he led his nation out of Egypt. In 538 B.C., an expedition of some fifty thousand Jews did go back to the Promised Land. But they didn't find life too promising in the devastation and ruin. They managed to rebuild the temple, but not without a great deal of trouble, particularly from their Samaritan neighbors to the north. (See Ezra 1-6.)

So things ground along for some eighty more years. Word of the problems down in Jerusalem got back to Babylon, where a great many Jews still remained. These Jews back in Babylon hadn't deserted the faith. They had simply adapted themselves to their new surroundings. Instead of worshiping in the Temple at Jerusalem they developed what they called the synagogue—sort of an outpost of the main temple—and there they still practiced their worship of Yahweh.

Life in Babylonia really wasn't that hard or oppressive. The Jews were not kept in chains. If they behaved themselves they were free to rebuild their lives and pursue trades and occupations.

Now suppose you are one of these second or third generation Jews born in captivity up there in Babylon. You have never known what it is like to worship in the Temple at Jerusalem. Oh yes, you've heard the old ones talk about it, but it's all rather unreal.

Let's say you become a leader among the deported Jews in Babylon. Your name is Eliezer and you are a priest serving in the Babylonian synagogue.

One day you hear of a request by a fellow named Ezra. You know of him—a Jewish scribe who is sort of Secretary of State for Jewish affairs in the Persian government. It seems he's heard about all the trouble they're having resettling Jerusalem and he has requested permission from King Artaxerxes to take a group of his countrymen down there for a firsthand look.

King Artaxerxes has not only granted Ezra permission to go; he's thrown in a travel allowance to finance the expedition. But it seems Ezra is short of men—particularly priests and Levites (keepers of the law). That's where you come in. You're just the kind of man he wants.

Comfort or commitment—that's Eliezer's choice

Attention loyal Jews: WE NEED YOU! Back to Jerusalem!

Ezra the Scribe

But is this the kind of adventure *you* want? Will it be worth it to be uprooted, to travel hundreds of miles across burning desert, risking your life to

147

bandits, wild animals, sandstorms and who knows what, all to try to help a bunch of "fanatics" who think it's important to keep the old traditions going? No one can blame you for pondering a few options.

Of course, if you are one of the Jewish zealots you probably won't even think twice. Many of your fellow Jews are living examples of Psalm 137 as they "weep in a foreign land," longing for the day of their return to Israel.

But suppose you don't feel quite that patriotic about it. Suppose all the oratory about "no good Jew wanting to stay in Babylon" doesn't impress you.

After all, look at the record. The first expedition of 50,000 Jews went back to Jerusalem 80 years ago. Yes, they have succeeded in rebuilding the Temple, but the reports coming back from Jerusalem are pessimistic.

The people aren't keeping the law; they are unhappy and almost ready for revolt. The rebuilt Temple is a poor imitation of the grandeur and splendor in the one Solomon constructed some 400 years ago. To be blunt the glory and the good life just aren't there.

Meanwhile, in Babylon the synagogue has become a new symbol of Jewish worship. With the synagogue you and your fellow Jews can maintain your faith in a foreign land. You can still approach God and worship in His house. You can remain a good Jew without having to locate yourself geographically close to Jerusalem.

And you aren't forgetting that business is good

Do Ezra's plans impress you, Eliezer?

IF YOU'RE THE PATRIOTIC TYPE...

WHEN DO WE LEAVE !? JERUSALEM FOREVER!

BUT IF PATRIOTISM DOESN'T GRAB YOU...

WHY GO BACK TO POVERTY AND DANGER JUST TO KEEP TRADITIONS GOING?

WE CAN WORSHIP GOD HERE IN OUR SYNAGOGUE. WHO NEEDS THE TEMPLE IN JERUSALEM?

BESIDES BUSINESS IS BOOMING

here in Babylon—the land where you were born and reared.

No wonder, then, that you and many other Jews might have real questions:

"Can the restored land of Israel survive?"

"Is restoring Israel even necessary?"

"Why can't I have faith in God right here in Babylon?"

To get the story on what Eliezer and his fellow priests and Levites did, turn to p. 168, or Ezra 8. But before you do, think through, perhaps even write out, just what you would have done had you been Eliezer and *why*.

If you stay on the human level—patriotic loyalty versus being practical—you miss the point. The real question is, "What are my *motives?*" Not all those who returned to Jerusalem went with the right motives. Some wanted adventure and excitement. Others had fanatical devotion to their country. Some hadn't made good in Babylon and they hoped the frontier would offer new opportunities.

But what about God? What did He want? What did He think? Why had He set aside the Jewish nation in the first place to be His "chosen people"? Why did He give them the land of Israel? Was the land of Israel a means or an end? Those were the questions facing Eliezer and other Jews in Babylon in 457 B.C.[1]

For believers in God today the questions are worded a bit differently, but they still ask the same thing:

"Where is the right spot for me? What is the right thing for me to do? Who is the right person

150

for me to join with—in friendship, in work, in play, in marriage, in employment?"

Decisions, decisions. We all have to make them. We can make them with God or without Him. The Bible promises that God will guide the believer.

"In all thy ways acknowledge him, and he shall direct thy paths" (Prov. 3:6).

"If any of you lack wisdom, let him ask of God . . . and it shall be given him" (James 1:5).

"When he, the Spirit of truth, has come, he will guide you into all truth . . ." (John 16:13).

But it's easy to misuse verses like these and develop a sort of vending machine Christianity. You insert your ten or twenty-five-cent prayer, on to which you tack an appropriate Scripture verse, and (supposedly) out comes the answer for what you're supposed to do tomorrow, next week or next summer.

But life isn't made up of neat little slots from which you receive pat answers. All too often, you run smack into a choice where the answer isn't clear at all. There are good arguments for and against doing something, going somewhere, taking a job, etc., etc.

There must be a better way. Cliff Richard, British teen-age singing idol, found it. Cliff committed his life to Christ during the Billy Graham evangelistic campaign held in England in 1966. In his book *The Way I See It,* he says, "I believe definitely that God does guide us, without a doubt, but perhaps not in the way people mean it who ask this question.

"The way I see it, the basic Christian commitment is to tell God you want to do things His way, not your own, in the future. You believe He has heard and answered that prayer, and so you accept *whatever comes* as being His will for you. Even if what comes is not what you expected or want, yet still God *is* guiding and it *is* His will.

"We may think we are choosing to do things, and we are; but God knows in advance what we will choose. If we pray for His guidance it shows we want to do His will and we are aligning ourselves with His plans for us. To accept that we are responsible for our actions, and yet God knows all about us and plans our lives for us, is hard. But to accept both these things is the basis of humility, giving *myself* to God. I am responsible, yet I am completely dependent."[2]

Does that sound a bit contradictory? Perhaps, but think about it and then decide if you'd rather do it Richard's way or if you want to catch the brass ring and ride the merry-go-round called "How do I find God's will?"

Maybe it's time for us to stop playing games and start admitting that we are bound to make mistakes. It is quite possible to be a Christian and make wrong choices about where you will work, what you will do—yes, even whom you will marry. It is quite possible to pray for guidance about taking a certain job, studying a certain course, or buying a certain item and then find that the situation doesn't work out at all.

Instead of coming up with a lot of sanctimonious sour grapes, why not just admit that you blew it? Admit it to yourself and confess it to God.

It may be that you made a dumb move. Maybe you made a selfish move and you didn't consult God as much as you thought you had. God permitted you to go ahead and make your mistake.

Allowing us to make mistakes is God's will for our lives, too. There is no question that He has a plan for us, a better way that we can go. But if we plan something else through error, human frailty, or just plain stubborn, sinful pride, He lets us do so.

Theologians call this God's "permissive will." Keep in mind, however, that what God permits us to do doesn't always match up with what He would like to have us do. God wants us to become everything we can possibly be. What you become depends on the choices you make. The basic choice, of course, is giving yourself to God in Christ. Next you have to take responsibility for your actions while still realizing that what you might do may not be what God always has in mind for you.

Does all this sound a bit dangerous? It certainly doesn't do much for the "guardian angel" idea. Why, to think that God would let you go ahead and do something that He doesn't want you to do sounds downright unloving on His part.

But realizing that God has given you freedom of choice, and that you're responsible for your choices, has its advantages. For one thing, the Christian life becomes less of a guessing game in which you measure your spirituality by how victorious you feel or by how well things have worked out.

153

... look for Christ and you will find Him... with everything else thrown in.[3] **C.S. LEWIS**

We often read the story of a missionary, minister or some other Christian leader who has been terribly successful. Because of all his "blessings," he is sure he is in God's will. But we seldom read stories about the people who wind up "unblessed"—the ones who run smack into all kinds of trouble, frustration, despair, divorce and even death. Somehow we don't like to write up Christian failures. We prefer to confuse the success syndrome with God's will and God's blessing.

In 1956 Elisabeth Elliot's husband, Jim, was one of five missionaries who ventured into the territory of stone age Auca Indians to tell them about Christ. All five men died at the end of Auca spears. *Life* magazine covered the story and the world gasped in dismay at the "needless waste" of five fine young men. Not much success here (although later Mrs. Elliott and other widowed wives went in and lived with the Aucas and led many of them to Christ). Perhaps it was this kind of experience that led Betty Elliott to write the following prayer . . .

THAT I MIGHT KNOW HIM

Lord, you have said, I AM THE WAY—

    not that we shall never be confused.

You have said, I AM THE TRUTH—

    not that we shall have all the answers.

And, I AM THE LIFE—

    not that we shall never die.

Teach me to know you here on earth—

    in its tangled maze of pathways,

    to know you as THE WAY;

    in its unanswerable mysteries,

    to know you as THE TRUTH;

    in the face of suffering and death,

    to know you as THE LIFE.

Thank you, Lord, for not offering us a method,

    saying, THIS is the Way.

Thank you for not granting us a set of invariable

    propositions, saying, THIS is the Truth.

Thank you for not delivering us from being human,

    saying, THIS is the Life.

Thank you, Lord, for saying instead, I AM, and

    for thus giving us yourself. [4]

Why not change the question to a declaration. Instead of asking "I wonder what God wants me to do," say, "Thank you, Lord, for yourself."

Then you can take the failures with the successes, *because you know there will be both.*

There's a mystery about it, sure enough. This mystery lies in the difference between. *wanting God,* not worrying about "being in His will." The more you want of God, the more of yourself you can share with Him.

How do you grapple with this mystery? Pray, *really pray,* and the Holy Spirit will give you answers you would never discover by yourself.

And then, "Lord willing," won't be a cliche you tack on the end of plans you have made all on your own. Instead, "Lord willing," will be written all over your attitude and actions.

Then you can relax. *If the Lord wants you to,* you will live and do this or that. And if He doesn't, you'll find it out and be able to accept it. It's your move.

It's my move

1. Thank you, Lord, for working things out so nicely in regard to _____

_____

2. Lord, you know things aren't working out too well for me in regard to _____

_____

Help me figure out where I "blew it."

3. Lord, you know I have to make a decision concerning _____

_____

Passages to remind me God is in control, but He still gives me freedom of choice: Romans 11:33-36; I Corinthians 8:6; Isaiah 55:8-11; Romans 8:28.

They made MORE than History

The Old Testament seems dry and dusty to a lot of people because they see it only as a book of Jewish history. Many people never sort out all of the Bible stories and get them straight. The Old Testament remains a confusing jumble of patriarchs, proverbs, prophets, good and bad kings. And did the Exodus come before or after the Exile?

What follows is no attempt to present a version of "the Old Testament made simple." But it may help to see the Old Testament as a continuing serial of sorts in which God and certain people are the leading characters. As you follow the adventures of these men you live through the ups and downs of Israel, God's chosen people, who lived out their lives in what one Bible scholar calls "the international arena of ancient culture."[1]

Christians call the Bible "God's plan of redemption." To redeem means that you "buy back or liberate by payment." In reference to God's dealings with men, redemption is concerned with freeing men from their slavery to sin.

It all started with Adam and Eve. They were doing nicely in the Garden of Eden when Satan popped up and whispered that they couldn't possibly get ahead in life without a good education. So, Eve had to taste the fruit off that certain tree of knowledge. And Adam went along with his wife in disobeying God's express commands.

From the fall of Adam and Eve in the Garden (Genesis

3) sprung the sinfulness of the human race. From the Fall onward God began working His plan of redemption—a plan to "buy man back" from the consequences of his own sin.

But things got so bad in those early (undatable) days that God decided to practically wipe the slate clean and start over. He sent the Flood which destroyed everything except Noah, his family, and the animals that Noah saved.

Most people remember the story of Noah and the ark from accounts heard in Sunday school as small children. Gen. 6:22 reports that ". . . Noah did all that God commanded him," but surely he must have had some questions and second thoughts when God asked him to build a giant boat out in the middle of the desert with no water within miles.

Noah had to have faith. He had to trust God enough to face the ridicule and scorn heaped upon him by his pagan, idolatrous neighbors.

Build an ark over three hundred feet long? Fill it with pairs of animals, birds, reptiles? Was Noah hearing things? He had always walked with God, living a righteous life, but could this be real?

NOAH had to choose: look like a fool or do as God asked.

But Noah went ahead and did as he was told. He built the ark and the Flood did come just as God promised (Genesis 7,8). All living things were destroyed except those saved in Noah's ark. And from Noah's sons—Shem, Ham, Japheth—came the repopulation of the earth (Genesis 9, 10).

Centuries later, Abram, a descendant of Shem, was living in the city of Ur in what is now Iraq. Abram was the son of Terah, an idol maker. God spoke to Abram and said: "Leave your own country . . . and go to the land I will guide you to. If you do, I will cause you to become the father of a great nation" (Gen. 12:1,2, "Living Books of

159

Moses"). Abram obeyed God and with his family journeyed hundreds of miles to the west, finally settling in Canaan, the land God had promised (Genesis 12).

At first, Abram and his family faced starvation, but later they prospered. Soon there was not enough of the best grazing land and water holes to support the herds owned by Abram and his nephew Lot (Genesis 13). One of the men would have to take his herds and flocks to rocky, higher ground while the other remained in the lush Jordan valley. Abram's faith was tested with a practical decision: "Take the best for myself or let my nephew have first choice?"

ABRAHAM (1890-1750 BC)² faced the old question: Do I come first or ...?

Abram settled for the higher rocky ground while Lot took the well-watered grazing land. Nevertheless, Abram prospered while Lot and his family met disaster on the plains of Sodom and Gomorrah. Just as God had promised, Abraham (God changed his name—Gen. 17:5) did become the father of a great nation—the Jews.

God continued to carry out His plan of redemption through Isaac, child of faith, born when Abraham and Sarah were 100 and 90 years old respectively (Genesis 17–22). Isaac married Rebekah and they had twin sons—Jacob and Esau. The clever Jacob eventually tricked Esau out of his rights to a double portion of the family inheritance, and Esau swore revenge. Jacob had to flee the country, and he went north to Haran where he settled down with his Uncle Laban and eventually wed two of his daughters—Leah and the beautiful Rachel (Genesis 24–31).

Twenty years later Jacob decided to gather his family and possessions and return to Canaan. As he drew near its borders he got word that Esau was approaching with 400 armed men (Genesis 32). Should Jacob run, fight or try to trick Esau into an ambush? Or should Jacob apologize to Esau, trust God and take whatever might come?

JACOB (1750-1650 BC) *had to decide:* "*Trust God or my wits?*"

On the night before he was to meet Esau, Jacob wrestled with his fears, his conscience and with God Himself. After a desperate struggle he yielded to God and became His man completely (Genesis 32).

Jacob went on to meet Esau and discovered his brother had long since forgiven him (Genesis 33). Jacob resettled in Canaan and God—continuing to work with His people—told Jacob that his name was now Israel and renewed the promise that He had made to Jacob's grandfather Abraham (Gen. 35:11).

Jacob had twelve sons. Joseph, one of the youngest, "lorded it over" his brothers until, fed up, they sold him as a slave to a caravan headed for Egypt. They told their father that Joseph had been killed by a wild beast. Jacob was grief-stricken, and that seemed to be that for the next twenty years (Genesis 37). Then famine hit Canaan and the brothers had to go to Egypt to buy grain.

Joseph, who had gone to Egypt as a slave, was now prime minister in charge of food distribution (Genesis 38–42). Joseph's older brothers did not recognize the smooth-shaven, Egyptian-appearing man before whom they bowed, but Joseph recognized them. Joseph wondered if he should take revenge or show mercy and forgiveness . . .

JOSEPH (1710-1600 BC) *faced the age-old temptation to get revenge ...*

Joseph does forgive his brothers but Genesis 42–45 describes how Joseph keeps his identity secret at first and "teases" his brothers a bit before finally telling them who he is. Perhaps he was buying time to decide just what he really should do.

After the brothers make a second trip to Egypt for more grain, Joseph finally tells them who he is and invites the entire family to move to Egypt.

And so Israel (Jacob) led his family into Egypt where they stayed after his death to multiply by the thousands (Genesis 46–47). Some four hundred years later, the rulers of Egypt became afraid of the increasing number of Hebrews. They enslaved the Israelites and tried to cut their numbers down by killing Hebrew baby boys at birth (Exodus 1). Born at this time was Moses, whose mother saved his life by deceiving an Egyptian princess into taking him to rear as her own child (Exodus 2).

Grown to manhood, Moses killed an Egyptian for persecuting some Hebrew slaves. He fled into the Sinai desert and became a sheepherder (Exod. 2:11–22). One day as Moses was herding sheep near Mt. Horeb a bush burst into flames, but was not consumed and a Voice said to Moses, "Go get my people out of Egypt" (Exodus 3). Moses was startled and afraid. One man against the might of Pharaoh's armies? The whole idea seemed impossible.

MOSES (1350–1240 BC) knew what "Mission Impossible" was like ...

After engaging in an excuse-ridden dialogue with God, Moses finally received enough assurance to go back to Egypt and let God use him to perform the impossible. With powers given him by God, he pressured Pharaoh into letting the Israelites go, and then engineered the "greatest mass escape" of all time (Exodus 5–14).

Plague after plague came upon the Egyptians until finally Pharaoh agreed to let the Hebrews depart (Exodus 4–12). He pursued them to the Red Sea and tried to corner them there. A miraculous parting of the water let the Israelites across but drowned the Egyptians when they tried to follow (Exodus 13,14).

The Hebrews wandered in the desert for two years, received the Ten Commandments at Mt. Sinai (Exodus 19,20) and came to the borders of Canaan. They camped and sent out twelve spies to find out what kind of country Canaan was. Among the spies were Joshua and Caleb. When the twelve returned, ten of the spies were extremely negative and told the people they could not possibly conquer the land (Numbers 13). Joshua and Caleb had other ideas, because they had faith in God's power. But the people were angry—disillusioned, and in no mood to be "talked into committing suicide." What would Joshua do?

JOSHUA (1250-1200 BC) was God's optimist, but...

When Joshua and Caleb, along with Moses and Aaron, tried to convince the Hebrews that with God's help they could conquer Canaan, the rebellious people threatened to stone them. Finally, God settled the matter by sentencing the Israelites to at least 38 more years of wandering in the wilderness (Numbers 34). Furthermore, God said that Joshua and Caleb would be the only ones of their generation who would be allowed to enter Canaan.

Years later Joshua did lead the Israelites into Canaan and "conquered the land"—but not completely. (See the Book of Joshua.) Then came the "dark ages" of Israelite history with every man doing "what was right in his own eyes" (Judg. 21:25). The Hebrews married the pagan Canaanites, worshiped idols, were attacked and persecuted by pagan enemies. "Dark ages" or not, God continued working with His people. Periodically He would raise up a "judge" to guide them out of their difficulties. (See the Book of Judges.)

Samuel, the last of the judges, did his best, but the Israelites demanded a king so they could "be like other nations" (I Sam. 8:5). Samuel knew a king wouldn't help, because the real problem was lack of faith and dedication to God. But if Samuel refused it would look like he was protecting his own "religious establishment." Samuel and Israel faced a dilemma . . .

SAMUEL (1050-1010 BC) and Israel faced a crisis . . .

God settled Samuel's dilemma by instructing him to anoint a king (I Sam. 8:22). God said in effect: "Let these stiffnecked, proud people find out firsthand what it will be like to be run by political machinery instead of being led by Me and the leader I would give them." (See I Sam. 8:10–22.)

So Samuel anointed Saul the first king of Israel (I Samuel 10). Saul enjoyed success at first, but after Saul's disobedience to God (I Samuel 13–15) the old prophet told Saul that God had rejected him and that his days as king were numbered.

At God's command, Samuel anointed a shepherd boy, David, to be king, but while Saul lived he would remain on the throne.

David gained tremendous popularity by defeating the giant Goliath in one of the best-known battles of all time (I Samuel 17,18). Saul, tortured by guilt and frustration, decided that David was "out to get him" and vowed to kill David. Jonathan, Saul's son, was temporarily successful in talking his father out of his murderous ideas. But Saul was soon after David again (I Samuel 19), and Jonathan had to choose between being loyal to his father or trying to prevent the murder of his best friend. He and David had sworn their love for one another in a lifelong covenant. Would Jonathan keep that covenant? If he let his father kill David, he would be in line for the throne . . .

JONATHAN and DAVID (1036 - 961 BC) were more than just pals...

Jonathan warned David, who escaped and became an outlaw, hunted by Saul's men (I Samuel 20–26). In the end Jonathan's choice cost him everything and he died with his father, hopelessly outnumbered by Philistine enemies (I Samuel 31).

After Saul's death, David became king of Israel and in time united the nation. His son Solomon followed him to the throne and built Israel into a prosperous and powerful nation. Seeking even more political power, Solomon married daughters of pagan kings (I Kings 2:11). His foreign wives brought with them pagan gods and so, while enjoying a record "gross national product," Israel rotted at the seams spiritually.

In addition, there was rebellion because of heavy taxes and harsh labor requirements. One of the chief rebels was Jeroboam, an official in northern Israel. Solomon tried to have the young upstart assassinated, but Jeroboam escaped.

After Solomon's death, his son Rehoboam took the throne and Jeroboam returned to challenge him for power by requesting lower taxes and less work. Older men on Rehoboam's council said "lower taxes" and give the people relief. Younger men urged Rehoboam to raise the taxes, to "be the boss" (I Kings 12:1–11). Rehoboam faced a decision that would have far-reaching effects on the entire country . . .

SOLOMON'S son REHOBOAM (968-911 BC) made one of the crucial choices in the Old Testament

King Rehoboam arrogantly raised the taxes, and his decision cost him most of his kingdom. Ten tribes seceded to become the Northern Kingdom (Israel) under Jeroboam. Rehoboam was left to rule over the Southern Kingdom (Judah) containing only two tribes (I Kings 12:21–24).

The Israelite people, once united under God, were now divided. For the next 300 years one king after another came to the thrones of the Northern and Southern Kingdoms. Most of these kings were weak and corrupt and the Hebrew people drifted further and further into idolatry (I Kings 14:16).

Nevertheless, God continued to work with His people. He sent prophets to remind the Israelites of His love for them and of their responsibilities to Him. The prophets also told of the judgments that would come as a result of their sin. One of the most outspoken prophets was Elijah, who appeared one day to confront King Ahab and his evil wife Jezebel with God's judgment (I Kings 17).

Jezebel, daughter of a pagan Phoenician king, had married Ahab, king of Israel, and she had tried to stamp out worship of Yahweh, the true God of Israel, and institute worship of Baal. A showdown between Elijah and Jezebel's pagan priests finally came on Mt. Carmel in a contest to see whose God would answer by fire when sacrifices were offered. Some 850 priests of Baal and Asherah prayed and shouted for hours, but nothing happened. Then Elijah's brief and earnest prayer was answered immediately with leaping flames. In the tumult that followed, people recognized God as Lord and 450 priests of Baal were executed (I Kings 18).

Queen Jezebel swore to have Elijah's life within 24 hours (I Kings 19:2). Elijah's friends deserted him and the courage of the mountaintop left him. Elijah had to decide to fight, run or simply be killed . . .

ELIJAH (900-850 BC) was a wanted man and so ...

Elijah did run—some 80 miles into the desert—where in despair he wished he were dead. But God's "still small voice" instructed him to go back to Israel and anoint Elisha to succeed him as prophet (I Kings 19:9–21).

Elijah obeyed and his successor Elisha had a powerful ministry, but the Hebrews slipped further into idolatry. By 800 B.C. both kingdoms—Israel and Judah—were caught in the middle of a battle for world supremacy involving Egypt, Assyria and Babylonia. (See II Kings.) In 721 B.C. Israel was overrun by the Assyrians. In the years that followed, the Babylonians conquered the Assyrians and then swept into Judah on their way to fight the Egyptians. They partially conquered Judah, but left Jerusalem intact with a puppet king—Zedekiah (II Kings 24).

Jeremiah, a prophet at that time, continually warned Judah of judgment for its sin. So disturbing was Jeremiah to the people that they ridiculed and beat him. Following the partial occupation of Judah, Hananiah, a false prophet, said that in two years Babylon's power would be broken and Judah would be f.ee (Jeremiah 28). Jeremiah knew this was a lie and he had to decide if he would contradict Hananiah's words, which sounded very good to everyone, or tell the truth and risk another beating and possibly death.

JEREMIAH (627-575 BC) was a prophet without honor, period!!

Jeremiah disagreed with Hananiah and suffered imprisonment and exile. But as Jeremiah said, the Babylonians did return. They sacked Jerusalem and took the strongest inhabitants captive (Jeremiah 28–52). The Hebrews spent 70 years in captivity and watched Persia conquer Babylon. Then Cyrus, the Persian ruler, decreed that all captives, including the Hebrews, could return to their homelands and an initial expedition of 50,000 Israelites did go back to the Promised Land.

Many of the Jews stayed in Babylon living in relative freedom and prosperity. Meanwhile, the Jews who had returned to rebuild Jerusalem sent back discouraging re-

167

ports. These reports inspired Ezra, a Jewish scribe high in the Persian government, to organize an expedition to go back and help reclaim the glories that once were Israel's (Ezra 7). Ezra sent out a request for his fellow Jews to join with him.

He particularly wanted priests and scribes—men such as Eliezer (Ezra 8). Eliezer and his countrymen had to decide. Did they want to go to a devastated land where life was hard? Many of the Jews felt they had a good life in Babylon. Why go all the way to Jerusalem to worship God in the main temple? Why not worship Him in the synagogues they had built in Babylon?

EZRA (434-400 BC) gave men like Eliezer a tough choice: comfort or commitment?

Eliezer and fellow priests and scribes did join Ezra in his return to Jerusalem, but only 1,500 pioneers went back with him (Ezra 8–10).

As the Jews struggled to regain and rebuild their land, they became more concerned about their faith and their God than being a strong political power. They studied the Scriptures and many stressed legalistic adherence to Biblical law. At this point the Old Testament ends (about 400 B.C.).

Politically the Jews remained weak as they struggled through the next 400 years—first under the domination of Persia, then Egypt and Syria. For a period following the Maccabean revolt against the Syrian ruler Antiochus, the Jews had almost 80 years of relative independence, but that ended when Rome conquered Jerusalem and Palestine came under Roman rule in 63 B.C.

But in spite of political uncertainties and upheaval, the national dream of the Jews remained the same. They saw themselves as God's chosen people. They still looked for their promised Messiah and that day when politically they would be a great nation.

Did the dreams and expectations of the Jews come true? Did God send the promised Messiah? The answers are in the next chapters of God's continuing plan of redemption—the New Testament record of the coming of Christ to save His people from their sins.

Sources and Notes

CHAPTER 1

1. Adapted from *The Best of Bill Cosby,* Warner Bros., Seven Arts Records, Inc., Burbank, Calif.

2. *Interrobang,* Norman C. Habel, Fortress Press, Philadelphia, 1969, pp. 13, 14. Used by permission.

3. Adapted from Argus Poster #183, Argus Communications, 3505 North Ashland Avenue, Chicago, Illinois, 60657. Sets of colorful, 12¼" x 18½" Argus posters, created by Patricia Ellen Ricci, are available in sets of twenty. Write for free catalog.

4. Adapted from *Extraordinary Living for Ordinary Men,* Sam Shoemaker, 1965, Zondervan Publishing House, Grand Rapids, pp. 28, 29.

CHAPTER 2

1. Adapted from Argus Poster #P-59. See note under chapter 1.

2. From the long-playing record, *Silhouette Segments,* 1967, by American Lutheran Church. Used by permission.

CHAPTER 3

1. Adapted from Argus Poster #104. See note, chapter 1.

CHAPTER 4

1. Adapted from *The Best of Bill Cosby,* Warner Bros. recording.

2. *Are You Joking, Jeremiah?* Norman C. Habel, Concordia Publishing House, St. Louis, 1967, p. 108. Used by permission.

3. Adapted from Argus Poster #112. See note, chapter 1.

CHAPTER 5

1. Scholars date Moses approximately 1350–1240 B.C. During this period the Bible does not give statements that can be positively pegged on known historical dates. As a result scholars allow a "margin of error" of about 10% in their calculations.

2. Adapted from Argus Poster #202. See note, chapter 1.

3. From the long-playing record *Silhouette Segments,* 1967, by the American Lutheran Church. Used by permission.

CHAPTER 6

1. *For Mature Adults Only,* Norman C. Habel, Fortress Press, Philadelphia, 1969, pp. 28, 29. Used by permission.

2. Adapted from Argus Poster #222. See note, chapter 1.

CHAPTER 7

1. See *Games People Play,* Eric Berne, Grove Press, Inc., New York, 1964, p. 87.

2. Adapted from Argus Poster #179. See note, chapter 1.

CHAPTER 8
1. From "If you're over thirty, here's what the kids think of you," *Canadian Magazine*, January 3, 1970.

2. Bible research tells us that in David's time a good slinger was deadly with stones weighing a pound or more. Judges 20:16 describes 700 picked men who could "sling a stone at a hair, and not miss it." Goliath was apparently unaware of David's skill with his sling, and as he stood there sneering at his tiny opponent he made a perfect target.

3. "Like talking to a wall . . .", *Focus on Youth*, Vol. 3, No. 1, Summer, 1969. Used by permission.

4. "Irrelevant Dialogue," David N. Harbaugh, 108 Carriage Drive, Pittsburgh, Pa.

5. Adapted from Argus Poster #152. See note, chapter 1.

CHAPTER 9
1. *To Resist or to Surrender,* Paul Tournier, John Knox Press, 1964, p. 16. Used by permission.

2. *To Resist or to Surrender,* Paul Tournier, p. 11.

3. *Interrobang,* Norman C. Habel, pp. 40, 41. Used by permission.

4. Adapted from Argus Poster #139. See note, chapter 1.

CHAPTER 10
1. Bible scholar William S. LaSor comments that many interpreters see the actual meaning of the Hebrew in I Kings 18:27 as suggesting that Elijah is wondering if "Baal has gone to the toilet."

2. Difficult to accept and understand as it is, the slaughter of the 450 prophets of Baal was partly in judgment for past murders of prophets of Yahweh and also a judgment on Israelites who had deserted God to become Baal's prophets, a crime punishable by death according to Deut. 13:1-5. *See New Bible Commentary,* Eerdmans, 1956, p. 315.

3. From the long-playing record *Silhouette Segments* by American Lutheran Church. Used by permission.

CHAPTER 11
1. See introduction to the Book of Jeremiah, *Harper Study Bible,* Harold Lindsell, editor, Harper & Row, 1964, p. 1107.

2. *Good Old Plastic Jesus,* Earnest Larsen, Liguorian Books, 1968, pp. 130, 131. Used by permission.

3. Adapted from Argus Poster #206. See note, chapter 1.

CHAPTER 12
1. There is evidence that Ezra's mission may have been during the rule of Artaxerxes II, making the date 398 B.C. See *Light from the Ancient Past,* Princeton University Press, 1946, p. 200.

2. *The Way I See It,* Cliff Richard, Tyndale House, Wheaton, Illinois, 1968, p. 80. Used by permission.

3. *Prayers of Women,* Liza Sergio, Harper & Row, 1965. Used by permission.

4. *Mere Christianity,* C.S. Lewis, Macmillan and Fontana Books, 1952, p. 188. Used by permission.

APPENDIX
1. *The Old Testament Speaks,* Samuel J. Schultz, Harpers & Bros., New York, 1960, p. 5.

2. Note that the dates given for each Bible character do not cover his entire life span but rather show approximately his period of service.